Henry Longhurst
ONLY ON SUNDAYS

Henry Longhurst, both as a broadcaster and as a *Sunday Times* columnist, was for many years the voice of golf in Britain.

ONLY ON SUNDAYS was first published in 1964.

SPORTSPAGES

Only on Sundays

by

HENRY LONGHURST

SPORTS PAGES

SIMON & SCHUSTER

A SPORTSPAGES BOOK

First published in paperback by
Simon & Schuster Ltd in 1989

SPORTSPAGES
The Specialist Sports Bookshop
Caxton Walk
94–96 Charing Cross Road
London WC2H 0JG

Simon & Schuster Ltd
West Garden Place
Kendal Street
London W2 2AQ

Simon & Schuster of Australia Pty Ltd
Sydney

British Library Cataloguing-in-Publication Data available
ISBN 0–671–69974–1

Printed and bound in Great Britain by
Richard Clay Ltd, Bungay, Suffolk

SPORTSPAGES

'The idea behind *SPORTSPAGES* books is very simple – to make available a range of the best in sports writing. They may be new books or reprints; fiction or non-fiction; the work of a writer or a player. They will be sometimes passionate, sometimes judicious, and often both in turn.

The ground rules for choosing books for the series are also very simple – they must be about some sport or another, though typically of course the best sports books are as much about life as about sport; they must be honest; they must be well-written and enjoyable reading; and I must like them.'

John Gaustad

Contents

Foreword

If I had gone to any other school than the one into whose playing field you slice your first drive at Royal Eastbourne, I might never have taken up golf, for I should not constantly have had my attention lured from Greek irregular verbs to the golfers silhouetted on the skyline and, even more enviously, to the young caddies, some of them only my own age, plodding along behind them.

In such trivial ways are our lives fashioned and I must say that I have always been grateful to Providence for guiding mine in the direction it did. Golf has indeed been good to me. It is a pleasant game played often in the most heavenly places and on the whole by pleasant people, who are at their pleasantest when enjoying each other's company at their club. This is the world in which I have done what I am pleased to call my work and I am truly thankful.

Though I am now no more than a fine weather golfer, I find that I have played in no fewer than thirty different countries on courses ranging from St. Andrews to a sand-patch island in the Persian Gulf. The game has taken me as far afield as Tokyo, Mexico City, Puerto Rico, Melbourne and Hawaii and always I am impressed that, whatever differences may lie between them in race, language or politics, people when they play golf talk and think the same language. The thoughts of the man who misses a four-foot putt in Japan are precisely the same as those of the man who does it in Timbuctoo. Golf is the Esperanto of sport.

To write about it, as I have every Sunday for the best part of thirty-two years, brings one a host of friends, to say nothing of innumerable correspondents whom one may never meet, and to anyone who is gregarious by nature, this is a blessing not to be measured in terms of money.

I can truthfully claim that I have been asked many times to assemble some of my *Sunday Times* effusions in book form and here they are, with my thanks to the Editor for permission to reproduce them. I can only hope they will give as much pleasure in the reading as they did in the writing.

H.L.

Clayton Windmills,
Hassocks,
Sussex.
September 1964

Halcyon Days

'Will . . . you . . . get . . . on . . . with . . . your . . . work, *Long'st*!' The words are inseparably associated with my earliest memories of golf, the speaker being the late Mr. L. C. Vaughan Wilkes, headmaster of the school into whose sunken playing-field you slice your first drive at Royal Eastbourne. From behind a pile of books one would be seeking relief from Greek irregular verbs by peering with furtive envy at the golfers on the skyline, and in particular at the boy caddies trailing behind them.

Looking back, I fancy that the headmaster may have been casting equally envious eyes in the same direction, for he was himself a stalwart of the club and a scratch player. His son, J. C. V., later Warden of Radley, played for Oxford in 1924–5.

The caddies, though we did not know it, were also subject to discipline. They were fined for all manner of offences (3d. for being 'caught without sponge'), and it pleases me to think that an article I wrote about them hangs framed in the clubhouse today.

The game of golf having thus entered one's consciousness at an early age and in the most favourable light, it was natural that one should wish to experiment with it. Having done so with some sawn-off clubs while on holiday at Yelverton, I was duly bitten with the bug, and for many years it became the abiding interest of my life during the holidays.

This was no bad thing, though in those days the game was frowned upon as lacking in 'team spirit'. Looking impartially back, I fancy this to have been nonsense, for how could a boy find twenty-one other boys and a pitch every day in darkest Bedfordshire to indulge in a team game?

At the risk of sounding pompous I should say that the frustrating, maddening game of golf can, in miniature, teach a boy, or a man, all the major lessons of life. Certainly there was no danger of becoming 'uppish'. There was no Golf Foundation to pamper the young in those days: only, as it seemed to me, retired Indian Army colonels with very white moustaches and very red faces, ever ready to chivvy any 'dam' boy' that got in the way.

To continue my personal saga, we come to one of those turning-points to which all of us can look back in our lives. In 1922 my parents took their holiday at Broadstairs and I entered for the juvenile tournament on the short course at North Foreland—age limit fourteen; handicap two strokes for every year below it. I was thirteen and my score of 65–2–63 (nine 3s, seven 4s and two 5s: I wonder if I could do it today) won the tournament. I was presented with the cup by Miss Phyllis Monkman, the actress, a member of the celebrated 'Co-optimists', wearing a fine feathered hat. I could not understand why, while I gazed with awe and gratitude at Miss Monkman, Miss Monkman gazed equally steadily at the camera.

Second, with 82–16–66, was Percy Belgrave Lucas, son of the secretary at Princes, Sandwich. He was still only six, and next day that sympathetic writer, the late R. Endersby Howard, wrote half a column about us. He recounted how, in a burst of fellow-feeling, I had offered to give my caddy a penny for every hole 'we' did in three, and my four-and-elevenpenny pair of white shoes, which he had admired, if we won.

This I did, and I have his letter of thanks before me now. His name was Frank Honour, and he was a boy of my age on holiday from Acton.

2

Of P. B. Lucas, future Walker Cup captain, possibly the greatest left-hander of all time and sometime Member for Brentford and Chiswick, Endersby Howard wrote: 'This was an astonishing performance for a boy of six. Standing about the height of a man's driver (42 inches) and dressed in a little grey jersey suit and white socks and shoes, he took complete charge of his father, who carried his clubs. 'Niblick' he would request imperiously when he hit the ball into a bunker; and his bunker shots were masterpieces of advanced golfing art.'

It was soon afterwards that I watched for the first time a Great Golfer, and, perhaps because he was the first, he has always to me been the greatest. Posterity will ridicule such a verdict but I still declare that if, blindfolded, I could listen to a dozen great players driving off, I could tell by the sweetness of the click which one was Abe Mitchell. The occasion was an invitation tournament at Letchworth and I still possess a picture of Mitchell thumping the ball from the 8th tee, with myself as a small boy just visible behind his flying coat-tails—little suspecting that within a few yards of this spot I was destined some years later to do my first hole in one.

As I had holed an 80-yard pitch at the previous hole, I have long claimed to be the only golfer in history to hole two successive shots with the same club without putting it back in the bag.

When the Old Carthusians were winning the Halford Hewitt tournament at Deal with such regularity in the 'thirties, it was often supposed that golf must have been encouraged at Charterhouse when members of the winning teams were at school there. This, however, was far from the fact. I went there within a few weeks of the red-letter day at North Foreland and for the first year or two one was not even allowed a bicycle. After that there was the chance only of an occasional game during the latter part of the Easter and summer terms (sorry, 'quarters'!), and this only the hard way by bicycling four miles each way to the West Surrey course at Enton.

Apart from a pre-war match against the school—as a result of which I regret to say that the club was put out of bounds for some years—and more recent visits on foot during the annual starvation-fortnight at Enton Hall nearby, I did not play at West Surrey again till last year. So little can we have played at school that I found that I did not remember the middle part of this delightful course at all.

Having passed, all unknowing, into what turned out to be the best college in Cambridge, or Oxford either for that matter, namely Clare, I found myself at the beginning of four years of unbounded bliss and delight, the buffer state between the impatient schoolboy and the grown-up responsible for his own fortunes and follies. Studiously attending the lectures at first (B.A.Econ.Cantab.: never mind what class!) I found my thoughts more often elsewhere. It was a year mercifully when there were a good many places to be filled in the golf team, but an unlimited quantity, so it seemed, of freshmen with fearsome reputations to fill them.

Only those who have played in the University trials have plumbed the full depths of nervous futility in golf. I managed to get a lift in a friend's sidecar to Mildenhall—a queer course it seemed: very different from Bedford—and, panicking from the start, got round, I think, in 84. Later I tied in a competition with the captain, Geoffrey Illingworth, won the play-off by a stroke, and was invited to play on the following Saturday against Worplesdon. My opponent, to whom I shall ever be grateful, played execrably: I won by seven and six, and thereafter hardly missed a match for three and a half years—and that is enough about myself.

To the University golfer life in those days was absolute heaven. I hope it is today, too, but I fancy that noses are kept more closely to the academic grindstone. For the two winter terms we had a match every Saturday and most Sundays, and I have never wavered in my conviction that golf was *the* game to have played. We became familiar with the finest clubs and courses, matching ourselves against some of the leading players of the day or against elders and betters who had earned distinction in many walks of life.

4

All were anxious to lend a helping hand, and many an undergraduate found his future being shaped through golfing contacts with his seniors. These friendships last a lifetime and one could have made them at that age through no other game.

To play golf for the University was, strangely enough, quite a rigorous business. In my first year we travelled mostly by train—7.47 a.m. from Cambridge, then across London to catch another at Waterloo or Victoria, and home by the last train, known, I regret to say, as 'The Fornicator', from Liverpool Street. Thereafter, however, we went by car—Marshall's Garage 6.30 a.m., and as likely as not a couple of inches of snow on the ground; breakfast at the Peahen at St. Albans, and an hour or more to drive after that.

Often our club opponents expressed astonishment that we should have already motored ninety miles. I remember how surprised I always was at this. Would one ever become so old and decrepit as to think it worthy of comment that by ten o'clock one had motored ninety miles in an open two-seater for a game of golf?

This was, of course, the golden age of motoring. You could get a 'runner' for £25 and a really reasonable car for £50; petrol was 1s. 2d. a gallon; and periodic refreshment at the Castle Hotel was calculated to convince Mr. Crack, the motor proctor's principal henchman, that he might well be mistaken in thinking it was your car he had seen racing through the village of Melbourne at half past eleven last Saturday night.

One of my companions was Billy Fiske who, as the first American to lose his life in the service of the Royal Air Force, is commemorated by a plaque in St. Paul's. Fiske had a super-charged $4\frac{1}{2}$-litre Bentley and was, I think, the finest and safest driver with whom I ever drove. He neither smoked nor drank, and his eye for speed enabled him for years to hold the world record on the Cresta. It was a poor day when we did not touch 110 m.p.h. on the long straight road to Mildenhall—after which, having covered the nineteen miles in seventeen minutes, he could never understand why his putting touch on the fast and tricky greens left something to be desired.

One evening in 1930 someone suggested: 'Why don't we all band together and go to that fabulous land of prohibition and plenty, the United States?' Most of us touched our fathers for the necessary £150, and Billy Fiske's father took care of those who could not. For this sum, incredibly, we travelled there and back on the old *Caronia* and played four universities and twenty clubs, in Philadelphia, Boston, and New York. It was, of course, a unique education, and not only in golf, for these were the days of gangsters, gin in the locker room, and 'knock three times and ask for Charlie'.

As captain I had the honour of playing Francis Ouimet at the Country Club, Brookline, where as a boy of nineteen he had made golfing history by beating the English giants, Vardon and Ray, in the play-off for the 1913 U.S. Open. It was the first of many visits to America, and began the accumulation of such a debt, by way of warm-hearted hospitality, that no man could hope to repay.

This part of the story shall close on a cold March day in 1931 on the eleventh hole at Sandwich. I like to recall that I had completed it in 3 with a drive, a brassie and a putt, but the pleasure at winning my single against Oxford was tempered by the sudden realization that these truly halcyon days, the only grown-up life I had ever known, were over. A great emptiness seemed to loom ahead.

After one or two false starts I joined a small, now defunct golf magazine—on a basis of 'three months for nothing, and then we'll see what we can pay you'—and exactly three months later, when it was clear that there was nothing to pay me with anyway, James Braid happened to mention to Sir Herbert Morgan that a young fellow who used to play for Cambridge had taken to writing about golf. As a result I was summoned to the office of the *Sunday Times* and lived happily ever after.

The Golden Age

The first man I watched winning an open championship was Gene Sarazen, and I can see as though it were yesterday this stocky, olive-skinned, smiling little man striding up the last fairway at Prince's, Sandwich, in 1932, at the head of an enormous crowd, accompanied by his ancient caddie, Skip Daniels—to whom he had become so attached that later he asked if he could come up and stand beside him when he was presented with the trophy.

Golfing writers, like critics in other spheres, may do their best to remain impartial but are bound to have their personal favourites, and Sarazen has always been one of mine. The son of an immigrant Italian carpenter, he was born Eugene Saraceni, and started his golfing life as a caddie—at the same club, strangely, as did Ed Sullivan, whose television show is now a national institution in the United States.

Ten years before, at the age of twenty-two, Sarazen had won both the open and professional championships in the States, and had then come to Troon in search of the British Open. He had started very early on the second qualifying day in a storm which kept the fishing-boats in harbour and sent waves crashing over the sea-wall beside the course. He took 85, failed to qualify by one stroke, made no excuses and endeared himself to all by saying, 'I will come back even if I have to swim the Atlantic.'

7

Together, perhaps, with Abe Mitchell he was the simplest golfer I ever saw. He stood with both feet rooted to the ground, grasped the club firmly in both hands with a couple of inches of shaft showing at the top, and gave the ball a tremendous, elementary thump. When I get fouled up in the mechanics of the game, which is more often than not these days, I can still produce a series of reasonable shots by forgetting the theories and imagining that I am Sarazen.

Perhaps it depends on how old you are, but the late 1920s and early 'thirties are regarded by most who knew them as the Golden Age of golf. This period produced great golfers who were also great characters. The courses they played, the problems they faced, were virtually the same as today (though until 1929 they had to master the game with hickory shafts), but they seemed to take their lighter moments more lightly and to delve more readily into aspects of life other than golf.

It was, to quote Sarazen: 'A nice slice of the century to be young in. The times were good, the parties were frequent, the girls were pretty, the drinks were long, and the stock market was strong as an ox.'

The greatest of the golfers-cum-characters was, of course, Walter Charles Hagen. (Could he conceivably have been the same figure, I sometimes wonder, if he had been known as Charlie Hagen instead of Walter?) He became regarded as the master-showman and, much as one may dislike it, I suppose this is a fair description of that part of his make-up that caused so many thousands to flock round with him. What magnetized them was not his good shots but his bad ones. He reckoned to play at least four atrocious strokes per round —and instantly to forget about them. His recovery shots were as impudent as his general outlook on life.

When he was presented with the £50 first prize for the Open at Sandwich, he handed it straight to his caddie—the same Skip Daniels.

Hagen, like Babe Ruth, became a legend in his lifetime. The stories they tell of him are legion and those that are not

8

true ought to be. Hagen getting Leo Diegel out of the clubhouse to watch him hole the five-yard putt to tie, in order to intimidate him for the morrow. . . . Hagen being admonished for staying up so late when his opponent had long since gone to bed and saying 'Yeah, he's in bed but he's not asleep.' . . . Hagen nonchalantly knocking in his final putt at Hoylake to win by one stroke and saying 'Sure I knew I had it to win—but no man ever beat *me* in a play-off.' . . . Hagen saying 'Who's going to be second?' and then winning—while imitators in search of the limelight said 'Who's going to be second?' and then finished twelfth.

Hagen set social and financial standards that were new to professional golf. He travelled in style, took a suite at the Savoy, and had himself driven in a hired Rolls-Royce. I remember the sensation he caused when he turned up, six hours late, at Porthcawl, complete with steamer trunks, cigar, and his son, 'Junior'. He twice took 81, but the crowd followed him to the end, content to be able to say they had seen Hagen play golf.

My last memory of him is at Carnoustie in the early hours of the morning with a basketful of trout in his hand. Lying well up in the Open Championship, he had just been fifty miles to go fishing.

So far as championship golf is concerned, the Golden Age was, for us in Britain, also largely an American age, though it was some consolation that in those days none of the great American players felt his fame to be securely sealed until he had won the British Open. In 1933 we managed to set them back in the Ryder Cup match and this and the Open Championship which followed were each characterized by a single stroke which I shall never forget.

The crowd which turned up at Southport and Ainsdale for the Ryder Cup may well have been the biggest seen in Britain to this day, though how many had come to see the golf and how many to see the Prince of Wales I should not care to say. At any rate, when the final scene was set, they seemed to be hundreds deep on the banks round the eighteenth green.

The match is all square; the last single is all square: Densmore Shute for America has missed his putt and taken five, and here is Syd Easterbrook with the very last stroke of the final day, the veritable golfer's nightmare, a curly four-foot putt with a left-hand borrow to win the entire match.

He holed it like a man, and I often wonder how many times he must have lived that moment in memory over again. Of all the shots I have seen in golf, that is the one I would most have hated to have to play.

Both sides went on to the Open at St. Andrews, where the Old course was burnt to a cinder and the ball left little puffs of dust as it pitched. At the long fifth there are two bunkers which the best of players often cannot carry with their second shot. Craig Wood *drove* into one of these and, losing a stroke, tied for the championship and lost on the play-off. This luckless stroke was later measured and found to be a few yards short of a quarter of a mile.

In the next year the long succession of American victories in the British Open came to an end. It was widely believed that Henry Cotton brought it to an end, but it is not uncharitable to say that this simply was not so, for the fact is that the Americans were not there. Cotton's finest hour was yet to come.

In the meantime, the burly son of an American Army officer, Lawson Little, was setting a new amateur standard at Prestwick. To reach the final his opponent, James Wallace, an artisan from Troon, had beaten no fewer than five Walker Cup players. His only reward was to go down in history as the victim of defeat by a record margin. I often find myself tempted to write of the 'biggest crowd I ever saw' but perhaps this really was it. The match had everything. Local Scot against great American . . . Saturday afternoon . . . and illicit free entry via the 'Aberdeen Gate' across the sand hills.

Little went round in 66 and was 12 up. He started the afternoon round with 3, 3, 4, 3, 3, and that was the end of that. He was escorted home through the crowd by a posse of

chequer-capped Scottish policemen, winner by two records—
14 and 13, and twenty past two.

The match was put forward an hour to enable him to catch
the boat for America and thousands of people were pouring
in long after he had said good-bye.

The Thomson-Locke Era

For fifteen years after the First War, the Open Championship was dominated by American golfers. In the years following the second, it has been dominated largely by two from the Commonwealth, Bobby Locke and Peter Thomson, each of whom has won four times. That formidable American pair, Hogan and Snead, have each won once, leaving only three years for Britain—in the persons of Daly, Cotton and Faulkner.

Cotton's championship at Muirfield, which I did not see through being for some reason in America, was marked by the visit on the second day of King George VI, whereupon the winner-to-be, suitably inspired, laid on a 66 for His Majesty's benefit—by two strokes the lowest individual round in the championship.

Of the other two, I remember, as so often, a single incident rather than the event as a whole. Daly, having out-putted the field at Hoylake, appeared to be home and dry, and late in the evening only the American amateur, Frank Stranahan, could conceivably catch him—and he needed a couple of threes to do it. This, at Hoylake, you simply do not get.

He duly took four at the seventeenth, but the huge crowd and the fact that this was almost the last shot of the day, lent an added drama to the scene as he played to the last green with two to tie. His ball, perfectly struck, soared up over the big cross-bunker, pitched on the green, rolled up towards the flag, and, to the biggest roar heard on a golf course for ten years, finished inches from the hole.

Faulkner won at Portrush and, as an inveterate toucher of wood and non-tempter of Fate, I can still hardly believe that the gods of golf allowed him to do so. At the end of the second day he was two or three shots ahead of the field and I can see him now, surrounded by a bevy of schoolboys and young ladies in search of his autograph.

'Open Champion, 1951,' he wrote—with two rounds to go. Someone asked him about his 'pencil-gripped' putter, which had received a good deal of notice. 'Oh,' he said, stretching his hands four feet apart like a fisherman describing the one that got away, 'I shall never miss another of *those*.'

I moved silently away lest fate mistake me for an accomplice and in some way give me the hammer, too. Nevertheless he went on cheerfully to win by two strokes.

Ben Hogan is a memorable man and, particularly since the motor accident from which he made so truly remarkable a recovery, a very fine one. He tackled the 1953 Open at Carnoustie as a personal challenge. After a none-too-happy experience as non-playing captain of the U.S. Ryder Cup team at Ganton four years previously, when he did not know whether he would ever play again, he had not wanted to come. He was persuaded, spent ten days getting the measure of this strange form of golf, and did four rounds, 73, 71, 70, 68, each of which was lower than the one before—a feat to which the records show no parallel except that of Jack White, of Sunningdale, in 1904.

Hogan's performance in the Canada Cup at Wentworth was equally remarkable but, to me, more human. Colossal crowds turned up and he sensed—I believe it made a great impression on him—that these good people not only wanted to see him play golf; they wanted him to win. He gave them the full treatment. He holed a chip at the first for a three and a putt for a two at the second, was out in thirty-one, holed a fifteen-yarder for a two at the tenth—and so had done his first *ten* holes in England in 33!

Our two Commonwealth 'monopolists' of the last few years, Thomson from Australia and Locke from South Africa, are as unlike as can be. Thomson's golf does not tend to produce dramatic moments. He always seems to drive down the middle; his seconds always seem to go on the green, and his putts always seem to go in the hole—and at the time it is very difficult to see any reason why they should not.

He is equable by nature and generally smiling. When he took seven at the fourteenth in his last round at St. Andrews, he played the rest of the round, to win, as though it had never happened.

How much more dramatic—though no more praiseworthy on that account, of course—was Locke's win at St. Andrews! A portly forty-one against Thomson's athletic-looking twenty-nine, he came up the last hole, attired in the familiar plus fours, white cap and white shoes, looking, as someone remarked, rather like the Archbishop's butler, and needing five to win. Aiming, as it appeared from behind the green, into the hotel dining-room on his right, he curved the ball up in a high parabola and dropped it with a plop a yard from the flag.

I suppose the biggest patriotic excitement in England since the war was the winning of the Ryder Cup two years ago at Lindrick, for which the utmost personal credit must go to David Rees for the spirit which he instilled into his team, whereby the Goliath of American golf was well and truly slain.

A strange quality of golf is the way in which a sense either of victory or defeat can convey itself to eight people playing singles in different parts of the course ten minutes apart. At Lindrick one could almost *see* it happening. The humble British turned like lions whose tails had been twisted long enough; the Americans disintegrated.

Nothing shall take away the glory, but, since these are personal reminiscences, I may be forgiven for saying that there were sundry unsatisfactory elements on both sides, and that the Ryder Cup match I really enjoyed was the previous one at the Thunderbird Club in the Californian desert. Here the air is like champagne, you can see a man riding a horse ten miles away, and the brilliant desert sunshine makes no costume and no combination of colours seem too bizarre. Grass grows lush and green, at incredible speed, and people cast aside all care. Celebrities like Bing Crosby and Perry Como ride their electric buggies unmolested—and a player on foot has no standing on the course!

They gave me a car, of course, the moment we got out of the aeroplane. Leaving the club one evening, I searched the gigantic parking lot and could not find it. All American cars look alike anyway, and with the wheel on the wrong side you cannot tell which way they are facing. I complained to a man in a white coat. He looked around. 'Aw,' he said, 'better take this one.'

'This one' turned out to be a lovely blue-and-white creation, on exhibition at the club, and bore a banner saying, 'You too can drive the new Chevrolet Bel-Air. Coming November 7'.

It had fifty-eight miles on the clock. I put this up to 580, left the car where I found it, and went on my way.

It was at Thunderbird, incidentally, that I met the man who has put all long hitters, past and present, into the background. The reason is simple. George Bayer is a perfectly normal first-class golfer. He hits it farther because he operates on a physical scale hitherto unparalleled. He is an enormous man. His hands in particular are enormous and make a 2-iron look like a matchstick.

I first met him and his wife sitting in a bar, where I remained standing and thus almost on a level. Later I watched him play. You find yourself standing with your mouth open. The first hole was 378 yards long; his drive pitched clean over it.

We Live to see the Day

It is natural to recall earlier open championships more vividly than those of the recent past, not so much, I like to think, because of approaching senility but because they were won by different individuals, whereas nowadays one has to sort out whether it was a Locke year or a Thomson year.

I find that the memory crystallizes sometimes on the finish, sometimes on the scene in general, sometimes on the man. In 1935 it was the finish.

Many people have one chance-in-a-lifetime and miss it by suddenly becoming afraid to win. Alfred Perry had his at Muirfield and took it as though the thought of losing had never entered his head. He used to slash at the ball with joyous abandon, and I have a film of him driving off for his final round. Whenever I show it, there is a momentary silence, followed by 'A-a-a-a-h!' and admiring laughter. In the end he needed two fives to win. At each of the two long finishing holes he disdainfully skirted the bunkers with his drive, slammed the ball to the heart of the green with a wooden club and knocked off a couple of fours as though in a summer evening fourball.

His oration at the prize-giving was a model of its kind. 'I'd rather play a round of golf than make a speech,' was all he said.

He was succeeded by Alfred Padgham, whose huge hands

enveloped the club as though it were a toy and who played with a serenity that I myself have not seen equalled. You didn't *worry* when you watched Padgham. The game, after all, was simple, especially the matter of rolling the ball into the hole, so why try to make it look difficult? He won every worthwhile tournament except one in 1936, including the Open at Hoylake, which he finished with a six-yard putt and no change of expression.

People often ask me what is the finest round of golf I have ever seen. I am not at a loss for an answer. It is 'Cotton's last round at Carnoustie in 1937'. What a day, and what a triumph that was! This time the Americans really *were* there —the whole victorious Ryder Cup team.

In spite of torrential rain Cotton went round this gigantic course in 71 to edge out poor Reginald Whitcombe, who had already been photographed as the winner, by two strokes. It was his finest hour.

That the great Whitcombe family should pass on without winning the championship seemed unthinkable but increasingly likely. I dare say, therefore, that when Reginald won at Sandwich in 1938 no win had ever given more general satisfaction. Such, certainly, was my own reaction, though for an added reason. When the last day began, such a gale blew up as had not been known in golfing history. By 9 a.m. the vast eight-masted exhibition tent had sunk with all hands. Steel-shafted clubs were twisted grotesquely into figures of eight; pullovers had already reached the sea a mile away.

In the last round only seven players broke 80, and four and even five putts per green were ten a penny. Padgham drove the eleventh, 392 yards, and got a two—and took four wooden-club shots to reach the fourteenth in the opposite direction.

In these conditions the simple two-fisted style of the Whitcombes came into its own and Reginald, his feet anchored to the ground, finished with 75–78 for 295. And I, through sundry wagers with friends on the Stock Exchange regarding the winning score, finished with what it would take £1,000 worth of honest toil to earn, tax free, today. It's an ill wind, indeed.

In the 'thirties I played a great deal of golf myself, accumulating gradually a 'score' of about 400 golf courses, so that it becomes increasingly difficult now to add a new one, but in all this varied and, I think, enviable experience I look back upon none with such nostalgic affection as the scene of the Halford Hewitt tournament, the Royal Cinque Ports links at Deal.

I realize now how incredibly fortunate I was. In the six years prior to the war the Old Carthusians won the tournament five times and were beaten in the semi-final in the other, so we saw the whole thing through, including the celebrations at the end, every time. On all these occasions it was my memorable lot to share a bedroom with Dale Bourn and play in the bottom foursome with J. S. F. Morrison.

Both were notable characters. Dale, I think it is fair to say, strayed from the fairway at times in life as well as in golf. He was rescued in the one instance by such charm of character that no one could be cross with him for long, and in the other by the fact that he always expected to be lucky, and was. Some of the strokes by which he won matches at the twenty-first hole—almost on the beach and tee-ed up on the only patch of grass in sight—left opponents gnashing their teeth and muttering that this really was too much.

Poor Dale! He was killed in a flying accident during the war. I often wonder what he would have made of the post-war world.

It would be idle to pretend that the partnership between Morrison and myself did not become something of a legend, though this was due almost entirely to the eccentricities of my partner, both on and off the course. In six years we were beaten only once—and that on the last hole when the main match was over—and I cannot help feeling that this was due partly to the amazement of our opponents at Morrison's methods and instruments.

He had been a tremendous athlete: cricket and football for Cambridge before the war and golf after it; full back for the Corinthians and Sunderland and captain of the Corinthians on the great day when they beat Blackburn Rovers in the F.A. Cup.

His golf, however, was far from athletic. He had a set of seven or eight clubs sprouting from a torn canvas bag and bearing little or no relation to each other, mostly of hickory and some with handles as thick as cricket bats. He was, however, an extremely crafty golfer and, though he often made a bad shot, he never made a stupid one. As Lloyd Mangrum has said, 'It isn't how. It's how many.' If our opponents did not believe it, they could always look in tomorrow's paper.

I am often asked if the story of Morrison and the taxi is true. It is. One morning we were drawn to play at 7.25 a.m., when the Goodwins lightship was still flashing in the Channel. We won easily and by 9.20 were in the Chequers, a small incongruous pub away out by the fourteenth. Here Morrison held court until he not only had to summon a taxi to come and fetch us in time for the next round but also ordered it again for the afternoon. I have always felt it to be poetic justice that on the fourteenth I missed a putt to win; Morrison missed on the next, and with the taxi, unbeknown to our opponents, following slowly along in the field beside the course we were taken to the eighteenth green.

The pious founder, Halford W. Hewitt, was himself a Carthusian. He was also, being rather pompous by nature, the perfect butt. If he sat down to read a newspaper in our sitting-room, it was automatic on the part of the man nearest him to light it. When he insisted on his evening game of bridge—he was very deaf—the nearest man conveyed the contents of his hand to the others. I dare say some of the most remarkable bids in the history of bridge were made in that sitting-room to get 'Hal' out all square.

It all sounds a bit schoolboyish now but, like the undergraduate before the magistrate on the morning after, 'I can only say, sir, that it appeared to be very funny at the time'.

From the ridiculous to the sublime the link is yet another Carthusian stalwart of those days, John Beck, who was chosen to captain the 1938 Walker Cup team against the Americans at St. Andrews. It was an honoured but unenviable task. Two years previously I had accompanied the team to Pine Valley and they had not scored a single point. (They had in fact halved three matches, but by the rather uncharitable practice of the day these were marked up as a nought to each side.)

Britain had never won the Walker Cup, and I came back firmly convinced that none of us would live to see the day when we did. The American team that came to St. Andrews was substantially the same that had made such nonsense of us at Pine Valley.

Our own team did not look particularly impressive on paper, but by the time the match began they were in tremendous heart. This was due to three influences. One was Beck's firm but amiable personal leadership. The second was James Bruen and the third was Cotton. Bruen, a young Irishman of only nineteen, was remarkable for the loop in his swing, whereby the club at one moment would be pointing almost directly over the tee box before 'righting itself' for the downswing. Seventy was rarely broken on the Old course in those days but Bruen started flashing round in anything from 69 to 66 and played eight consecutive rounds, the worst four of which would have won any open championship yet played at St. Andrews. The rest of the team responded to this new standard. Where 73s would have done before, they started going round in 70.

On Cotton's arrival, Beck at once incorporated him to play with and encourage the team. Cotton was absolutely in his prime, and it was quite impossible to play with him in those days without playing better oneself. Furthermore, vast crowds followed him whenever he turned out and the Americans for once practised almost in obscurity. 'Mirror, mirror, on the wall?' Could the answer really be 'The British'?

In the event it was—but how near a thing and what palpitations were to be endured before that memorable final scene! The match was all square with three singles to come in. Charles Stowe won by 2 and 1, Cecil Ewing was known to be two up and Alex Kyle, known to be leading, was away out in the country.

But here now was Ewing all square with two to play. He closed the Americans out with a four at the Road Hole and the whole world, it seemed, surged round him and his opponent, Ray Billows, on the last green. There was a great silence, but it was broken by a cheer from afar. Kyle was walking in and all was over.

The irrepressible Charlie Yates, of Atlanta, led the crowd in a rendering of *A Wee Doch-an-doris* from the steps of the Royal and Ancient, while inside an elderly member, pressing the bell, was heard to say 'Well, we've lived to see the day. *Steward!*'

So Much Flak

The more I see of other games and sports, the more I am struck by the similarity of their underlying principles and psychology with those of golf. The thought comes to mind because one or two kind friends have in the recent past invited me to help in slaughtering their pheasants—though that is perhaps an optimistic term regarding my own part in the proceedings. I like to think I generally succeed in making them swerve, or at least fly faster, but can never quite get out of my mind Osbert Lancaster's war-time drawing with the caption 'I suppose you realize, Sir Henry, that to the pheasant you and I are just so much flak'. Still, it is an exhilarating and provocative pastime, alternately luring you, like golf, into a ludicrous idea that you have 'Got it at last', then casting you back into the depths of humiliation and despair.

Twice in my life momentary success has set me secretly thinking, 'I shall never miss another of those'. Yet my last memory, as we left the field of battle near Mildenhall the other day, is of firing ten shots at five pheasants, all flying, as we used to say in sterner anti-aircraft days, at a 'constant height, course and speed', and not a single feather floating down from any one of them.

At golf you do have one indisputable advantage. You may slice it out of bounds over the railway line and be very angry indeed, but at least you can see where the damn thing went. If you know you are slicing, at least you can lay on such anti-slice precautions as you may be aware of next time—but when you fire ten carefully aimed shots and absolutely nothing happens whatever, it is as though you hit your drive up the middle and the ball vanished in mid-air. It makes you feel like throwing the offending weapon to the ground and walking in.

Shooting men, like golfers, are tremendous theorizers and I like to egg them on in this, partly because I am genuinely interested and partly because it restores my morale to find that in most cases even the experts have practically no idea what they are talking about. I usually set them going by recalling an occasion when I found myself standing in a deep Berkshire valley beside Mr. J. Arthur Rank. This gains me a good deal of face because Mr. Rank is a very distinguished performer, about plus-one, I should say, and to reveal that one has been firing in his company is like letting fall casually 'When I was playing with Cotton the other day . . .'

At any rate the pheasants shot across the valley as though jet-propelled, at what seemed about 1,000 feet, and though I put up a continuous barrage it resembled the early days of the blitz—more calculated to sustain civilian morale than do damage to the enemy—the targets being palpably out of range. I observed with chagrin, however, that around Mr. Rank they were falling from the sky like the leaves of autumn.

Unworthy thoughts, so familiar to golfers, flashed through my mind: he must have a better set of clubs, or maybe some new-fangled shafts, hot from America, or patent grips, or a lump of lead in the driver, or perhaps he was playing with the bigger ball or something.

In both pursuits the heart cry is the same—'What do I do to get length?' Ted Ray's immortal answer 'Hit 'em a —— sight harder, mate' will not do in respect of shooting. Perhaps, as I suggested to the experts, it lies in the cartridges—just as everyone believes golf professionals play with specially wound balls? Yes, says one man, I expect he gets them specially loaded. No, says the next, I remember old so-and-so

used to bring them down from 50 yards with No. 8s. . . .
Choked barrels, then, perhaps? If so, why don't they have
both barrels choked? Perhaps they do . . . or the length of
barrel maybe? . . . Ah, now you are nearer the mark. . .
Then why do some scratch players have these stubby little
22-inch barrels? . . . Oh, go away and play.

After much argument about it, I come out with my mind
assured on one point. As a golfer, I may waggle the glistening
clubs in the pro's shop and, even at £4 a club, be sorely
tempted, but in shooting a new set might cost me, I learn,
some £500. So the ancient blunderbuss will have to go on. I
suppose the only answer, to adapt Ted Ray, is 'Point it a ——
sight straighter, mate'.

Ice and Jungle

One of the indisputable characteristics of the Scottish race is that, though the municipal golfers of Glasgow may be staging a month's strike—by a coincidence the month least suitable to golf—against a charge of a florin per round instead of a shilling, nothing can prevent their brethren from carving out golf courses in the farthest distant parts of the world in places designed by Providence, one would have thought, for almost any other purpose. In sand and desert, boulders, jungle and snow there are at this very moment energetic Scotsmen scratching away at the surface of the earth with their niblicks.

Two instances have recently come my way, both from friends last met in Singapore. One, an ex-brigadier doctor, settled there after a distinguished military career in Burma, but uprooted himself last year to seek his fortune in Canada. His present practice in Alberta encompasses several thousand square miles, and among his patients are isolated Eskimos of the Western Arctic. Landing to visit them on some barren inhospitable island the other day and clambering over the rocks and ice, he looked down and beheld, of all things, a golf ball.

The Golfers' Handbook carries an intriguing item entitled 'Balls in Strange Places'. These include the ear of a donkey, somebody's drawing-room fire via the chimney, and the nests of wasps, larks, solar geese, pheasants and squirrels.[1] Bizarre though they may be, 'Arctic island apparently uninhabited by white men' must surely qualify for future inclusion. The answer, of course, was—Scotsmen. The number of holes had coincided with the number of members: three holes, two Scottish engineers and a Jesuit priest.

By these standards the Christmas Island Golf Club in the Indian Ocean is almost a tropical St. Andrews. Here the inhabitants consist mainly of 2,000 Chinese and thirty-seven Australians, of whom thirty-five were so ignorant, until twelve months ago, as never to have played golf. The arrival of another Scottish engineer, Mr. Frank McRae, soon corrected this lamentable state of affairs and within a matter of weeks the Europeans, having done their day's work for the Phosphate Company, were to be seen with bulldozers and axes clearing nine holes in the jungle.

My informant, a Singapore police officer visiting Christmas Island on an official mission, was much impressed with the result of their efforts. 'It is in a lovely position,' he says, 'with the sea and a 100-foot cliff on one side and dense jungle on the other. Great frigate birds wheel around you while you are playing, as though they had never seen such antics.' Everyone carries a T-shaped piece of wood to smooth away not only the stones but the crabs, which at this season migrate from the jungle to the sea to lay eggs. 'Literally tens of thousands,' he says, 'move down like a red carpet across the course. They are a sad hazard on the greens.'

He encloses a card of the course which shows it to measure 1,784 yards, with a bogey (I am glad the abominable 'standard scratch score' has not penetrated to the Indian Ocean!) of 31, but I am 'not to scoff at par-four holes of 180 and 192 yards. Think of the crabs! Peter Thomson would I am sure, be pleased with a 64 for 18 holes.'

Partnered with an ex-hockey player who still had the two games somewhat mixed up but was 'acquiring all the elements of untruthfulness of the seasoned campaigner', my

[1] See also 'Caddies, Clerics and Cows', page 58.

26

friend entered for a greensome tournament, which for some unaccountable reason is called a Canadian foursome in those parts. Their card of 37-nett was an easy winner but they were disqualified on the ground that he 'was not a member'.

Enterprising publishers of golf books in this country may note that in Christmas Island they have a sure, if microscopic, market. Tommy Armour's *How to Play Your Best Golf All The Time* is the only one so far to reach the island. Everyone now has his own copy and in some cases husband and wife have one apiece. There remains, however, great confusion about the rules, more particularly our old friend about hitting the pin within 20 yards, and I am begged to despatch a copy of the latest version forthwith. After much consulting of reference books in the local Post Office and discussion as to whether Christmas Island was 'one of ours', a copy is now on its way to Mr. McRae. Re crabs, I can only deem them an outside agency and therefore a rub of the green—unless of course they burrow, in which case see Rule 32 (1).

'Sergeant-Major' Sheridan

The Committee of the Sunningdale Golf Club in 1955 conferred upon a singular man a singular honour, unique so far as I know in the history of golf. They summoned their caddie-master, Sheridan, and, handing him a club tie, declared him an honorary member. In thanking them he remarked quite irrelevantly but, as all who have known him will testify, with perfect truth, 'Ah well, I've been making my own rules and regulations around here for forty-five years now'.

Sheridan started at Sunningdale as a young fellow in his early twenties and grew rapidly into an 'institution'. He came from the neighbourhood of North Berwick and his accent, despite nearly half a century amid the sophistication of Ascot, continues uncompromisingly to proclaim the fact.

The number of people who have waited in his little office, scanning surreptitiously the highly coloured and provocative picture postcards with which the walls are decorated, while Sheridan explains that there isn't a caddie and how anyone at that hour of the day could ever have expected that there would be defies his comprehension, must now run into thousands. They included for many years the Duke of Windsor, than whom no one, I am sure, will hail the honour done to Sheridan with greater acclaim.

Sheridan's assurance that no caddie is available has, for the twenty-seven years I have known the club, been instant and automatic. Once this preliminary gambit is over, it becomes a war of nerves. Weaker brethren go off muttering, carrying their clubs or fixing up a trolley. The stronger-minded leave their clubs leaning against the office and without further comment retire to the club-house, peering out from time to time to note that they are still there, unattended and ignored.

As the crisis nears, only those with years of experience have the nerve to make the correct move, which is to march out of the club-house and, turning the head neither to the right nor to the left, to proceed through the little iron gate, passing within two feet of the clubs, and thence, without a single backward glance, to the 1st tee. From here an occasional apprehensive glance may go undetected but the master hand does not descend to it. He remains with his back to the office, facing nonchalantly up the first fairway. Meanwhile, the party in front have driven off and departed. One's partner and opponents have all got caddies and one of them has actually teed his ball. This is the acid test. Survive it—and you've won. All the same, as the Duke said, it was a damned close-run thing.

As a 'character' Sheridan has accumulated around him over the years a crop of stories, many unprintable, mostly apocryphal, which invited instinctive comparison with an equally outspoken Scot, the late Andra' Kircaldy.

One of the oldest golfing stories is of the *nouveaux riches* who drive up to the club and inquire of the most influential member whether he is the caddie-master. 'No,' is the reply, 'but I happen to know that he does not require any caddies today.' It used to be told of 'Pa' Jackson at Stoke Poges and 'Aber' (J. F. Abercromby) at Addington and doubtless many others. If it ever did really happen, I am sure it was Sheridan.

Nevertheless, his bark is worse than his bite. No club has more teen-age caddies than Sunningdale and no one does more to help them start their golf than Sheridan. The

Sergeant-Major Brittain[1] of the caddie world, he first frightens the life out of them, then presents them with an old set of clubs to start upon. He helps to set them up in permanent jobs and, when times are hard, he buttonholes the members on their behalf with 'Come on, I want a quid out of you!' It is a bold man who does not reach at once for his wallet.

[1] Mr. Brittain was a Regimental Sergeant-Major in the Guards with a stupendous voice and a national reputation, who even played the part of himself in a film comedy. Officer cadets lived in great fear of him. 'I call you Sir and you call me Sir,' he used to tell them. 'The only difference is that you mean it.'

Back to Nature

I often wonder what those ancient worthies who played the original golf amid the sand dunes of Scotland, playing the ball where it lay and improvising shots with their 'rut irons', would think of the sophisticated version we know today—the flawless fairways and greens; the sand bunkers so carefully raked as to present, to anyone who cares to learn it, the easiest shot in the game; the shining armoury of clubs, the supercharged balls and all the rest of it. The thought occurs the taxi the day before, to be standing on the 1st tee in the original version and have greatly enjoyed its primitive simplicity.

The scene was the Tripoli Golf Club, and a nice change it made, after picking one's way through snow-drifts to reach the taxi the day before, to be standing on the 1st tee in the sunshine beside the blue waters of the Mediterranean. The fairways on this links—and links it certainly must be called, for if ever there was a 'seaside' course this is it—consist of sand, stones and boulders, interspersed with a tiny species of daisy and a creeping blue flower that I took to be gentian. The greens are somewhat darker and firmer, the sand having been mixed with oil, and they are raked in circles, the hole thus resembling the bull's eye in the middle of a target.

The match was between Her Majesty's Ambassador, who holds the record for the course—one hour and eight minutes, playing by himself—and the Controller of State Properties on the one side and the officer commanding the British Military Mission to Libya and myself on the other. The Controller of State Properties, who hails from Llandrindod Wells, is the champion of Libya and would, I think, beat the better ball of Hogan and Snead on their first attempt, having mastered the art of causing the ball to lodge on the green from 100 yards. Orthodox methods, one soon learns, do not effect this. If you pitch short, the ball stops dead with a splash of sand. If you pitch on, it flies over the back as though off concrete.

We managed to halve with the champion and his distinguished partner, largely through my brilliant three at the sixteenth, which was brought about by one of the most remarkable putts ever made in North Africa. The green sloped sharply to the right and a strong wind was blowing from the left. I putted, from off the green, well to the right and in the last few feet the ball turned steeply up the slope and against the wind and ran into the hole.

On grass this might be held to be an optical illusion. On sand the evidence is there for all to see, the path of the ball marked clearly on the green. This always intrigues me, for it shows what a lot of nonsense is talked about top spin and such like. On a five-yard putt the evidence is that the ball does not touch the ground at all for the first yard and only touches it at intervals for the second yard. You can stand there all day, trying every kind of method, and still fail to make the ball leave a track along the ground from the moment you strike it.

Once you forget the unorthodoxy of playing golf without a blade of grass—which, strangely, you do in the first ten minutes—Tripoli has some very fine holes, at least two of them strongly reminiscent of home. The first, for instance, with the tree beside the shore and the sea sloping away in a little bay, is an almost exact replica of the first at Porthcawl. The fourth, where, having turned inland by the tunny-fish factory—mercifully not working at this time of year—you turn again and play straight out to sea, is the spit image of that wonderful hole they call the White Rocks at Portrush.

The tenth, curving along with the sea, needs only grass to make it one of the world's great holes. The view looking back along the shore to the distant city as it juts out into the sea, dazzling in the winter sun, absolutely takes your breath away.

A little farther on is the Underwater Explorers' Club, of which the Ambassador is an enthusiastic member. From time to time a periscope appears off-shore from the tenth, signifying that His Excellency, with his snorkel apparatus, is in surreptitious search of golf balls. His score this year so far is five.

Royal Benghazi

Your correspondent now finds himself, of all places, at Benghazi, in the alternate capture, loss, and recapture of which battered city so many readers will have played a memorable, if not wholly enthusiastic, part. The shell-pocked walls and gaunt skeletons of bombed buildings still bear silent witness to their activities of a dozen years ago. How they did it I cannot fathom, for the climate, perhaps in contrast to what we were enjoying at home when I left, enables me to remain awake only for two or three hours in the twenty-four.

It was not long, of course, before I found myself on the links of what the more patriotic members call the Royal Benghazi Golf Club—largely, I gather, on the ground that the Queen of Libya had a beach hut not far from the clubhouse. The nine-hole course—5,192 yards, bogey 72, and I lift my hat to anyone who can do it in that figure—is on true 'linksland' between the Mediterranean proper and the inland salt-water lake and is at this moment in the peak of condition, there being a suspicion of greenery on many of the fairways.

Closer inspection reveals this to consist mainly of little flowers like scarlet pimpernels. There are also a miniature edition of the rushes at Westward Ho!, but they are liable at any time, if the wind is in the wrong quarter, to vanish beneath the sand.

Nevertheless, whoever laid out the Benghazi golf course has contrived to create, out of some of the most unpromising material on the surface of the earth, some remarkably fine holes, and more than once, especially from the tee, one had the illusion of driving over the sand dunes at Sandwich or Deal. In one sense Benghazi has the advantage of these rather more celebrated courses. When the sea submerges it to a depth of three feet, as it does from time to time, the water simply sinks into the sand, thereby much improving the condition of the fairways.

The more I see of this desert golf, the more I feel it would do everyone good occasionally to play it. The ideal in modern 'civilized' golf, even among the more modest performers, seems to be to achieve a single 'grooved' swing to be used on all occasions and with a series of standardized clubs. Playing in the desert you can standardize nothing. You have to make it up as you go along. It brings back the original purpose of the game, which was to start at A and finish at B, encountering all manner of hazards on the way and overcoming them as best you might. It also rubs in the bitter truth that, if you cannot do it with five clubs, you certainly cannot do it with fourteen.

The enthusiasm here is tremendous. Golf is not a business to be taken lightly at the Royal Benghazi, where the English are outnumbered by Glasgow by approximately ten to one. We were preceded round the course by the semi-final of the foursomes tournament, a tense affair with no quarter asked or putts conceded. Two up with three to play and with a stroke at the sixteenth, one of the participants 'had only' to chip on to the green, or rather the brown, but had over-teed his ball in the sand and fluffed it a yard—a shot which I know only too well, having done it not less than twenty times.

The victim, having lost the match, sat lugubriously among the throng in the club-house, looking up occasionally to observe: 'I could have done it wi' ma putter.'

Another member, having described the house to which he proposed to retire on the edge of a Hampshire course, added solemnly, 'I have given my wife a power of attorney that, if the time comes when I can no longer play golf, she is to send for the vet and have me put down.'

Amid company thus dedicated I was gratified as well as astonished to see, on the board recording the club's trophies and prizewinners, my own name. I thought for a moment that it must be my namesake, the actor, on whose performances on TV and screen I am often congratulated, but it turned out that this was a prize that I had once contributed to the club through a friend.

It occurred to me that, while any fool could donate it, it would take a pretty alert and determined performer, in this company, to win it.

Bill of Rights

The essence of a biography is to make the reader feel that he has lived another man's life, sharing his hopes and disappointments and penetrating the workings of his mind, without the trouble and inconvenience of doing so. This standard is certainly achieved in the case of Norman von Nida's *Golf is My Business* (Frederick Muller) which was written in conjunction with an Australian journalist, Muir Maclaren.

The story of a life dedicated to competitive golf opens with a passage characteristic of both Von Nida and Hagen. Von Nida, aged fifteen, undersized, under weight, but perky as a bantam cock, is to caddie for the great Hagen at Brisbane. He is about the size of Hagen's bag. 'That's all right, Mr. Hagen,' he says, 'I am the best caddie in Brisbane.' 'O.K., son,' says Hagen, looking down at him. 'Then you and I are a pair, because I'm the best golfer in Brisbane.'

Von Nida came up the hard way. He was flung 50 feet from the Victoria Bridge into the shark-ridden Brisbane River, narrowly missing some electric cables, to deter him from walking home with another young gentleman's girl, and thereafter worked in various abattoirs, up to his knees in entrails and splitting sheep skulls with his bare hands—a practice to which he attributes the strength of his golf grip and possibly the meaty contents of his book. It was golf that rescued him and led him out into the fresh air to a life of

OOS–D

travel, good company, and success—golf and his passionate, combative determination to win.

What makes his book so refreshing is its frankness, not only about other people but about the incessant 'incidents' in which he has allegedly been involved. One of his principal targets, I have to reveal, is golf writers—for whom it is salutary for once to be on the receiving end. 'Most,' he thinks, 'are honest, but some are prejudiced, some careless and quite a few dishonest.' Leonard Crawley and Henry Longhurst 'are both sound and knowledgeable when they concern themselves with the play' (ah!), 'but are too often influenced by the demand for sensationalism which seems to be the bane of modern sports writers.' (Oh dear!) Elsewhere I get to myself, 'what tripe some golf writers indulge in!' But Crawley also, I am glad to see, gets a similar hon. mention on his own.

Von Nida has gone through life looking for his 'rights', as he calls them—and, one is inclined to suspect, for anyone who might be disposed to deprive him of them. One of the better examples, not mentioned in the book, was his perfectly serious claim during *The Daily Telegraph* foursomes, when his partner, J. C. Wilson, twice left him in a bunker, 'a man's entitled to be got out of a bunker'!

'I have never shrunk from speaking up for my rights,' he says, 'or trying to right what I considered wrong.' It is this, I think, which has been responsible for getting his name in the papers for so many extra-curricular activities. At Sunningdale he sacks his caddie for commenting unfavourably on his play and at St. Andrews for giving him the wrong line—as a result of which he has to wire for a caddie from London. At home he accuses Sarazen's manager of cheating him, Ed Oliver of playing the fool and putting him off, Tommy Bolt of being rude and 'bellyaching to Press men'.

Within days of his first arrival in America he is rolling on the ground by the scoreboard, locked in deadly combat with a professional who had palpably cheated, and is pulled off by a sheriff.

He falls out with the P.G.A. in Queensland and may not

perhaps endear himself to them here by calling the Ryder Cup 'a fiasco until Dominion players are admitted'.

All this is good strong stuff and does no one any harm. Our hero does, however, go on to say that the 1953 Ryder Cup at Wentworth, at which he was not present, was 'badly organized. . . . Nothing done to make the spectators comfortable. . . . Marshalling of crowds, catering, normal facilities non-existent.' As this was quite the best-run tournament in Britain up to that time and as Wentworth are determined that the Canada Cup, in which he is playing, shall be the best-run of all time, an apology to the captain and committee by today's post seems indicated. Its arrival would coincide nicely with the publication of the book.

Nevertheless, this is a brave book. It represents yet another blow by an at-heart likeable little man in a black beret, constantly misrepresented, misreported, misunderstood, labouring under the burden not of a chip on one shoulder but a tree trunk on both. The only man, in fact, not out of step.

Point of no Return

The opening of the new club-house of the Bedfordshire Golf
Club and the fact that your correspondent's bed recently fell
through the bedroom floor—thus disclosing a display of dry
rot and inedible fungi unparalleled in the experience of the
local health officer, he said, with the possible exception of a
case which had come his way some years ago at Plymouth—
may on the surface appear to have little connection with each
other. On the other hand, the cottages in which I live between the two windmills are mostly made of wood, and so
was the old club-house at Bedford. They say it took only
three hours before it was reduced to ashes and the insurance
fell due. If in the near future a glow suffuses the crest of the
South Downs not far from Ditchling Beacon, it will signify
that the temptation has proved irresistible.

As against that, the members of the Bedfordshire Club had
to content themselves for the best part of three years with a
couple of Nissen huts, and this, on the top of the Downs in
winter, is a prospect calculated to make the most militant
fire-raiser put the matches thoughtfully back in his pocket.
The insurance company may in this case breathe again.

Still, the club that rose again from the ashes at Bedford
was worth waiting for, and to be invited formally to declare
it open at the celebration party last week was to me not only
a great honour but a sentimental occasion. I remembered, I

remembered, the course where I was born . . . but to play on it again, in a competition for the aptly named Ashes Cup for which the members will play on this day every year, was a most humbling experience.

It is common knowledge that to revisit the scenes of one's boyhood reveals a most remarkable shrinkage in physical things, and this was no exception. Can this brown and turgid stream, for instance, no wider, it seems, than the Basingstoke Canal, be really the same Great Ouse on which I spent an idyllic Wind-in-the-Willows childhood? Can this modest row of poplars be really those whose slender tops I used to think (with the poet) were close against the sky?

The golf, however, brought a rude awakening. My thoughts went back to the small boy in the corduroy breeches battling with the long first hole. A good brassie might bring us somewhere near the dip, and a full spoon might then, with luck, clear it and land on the green for three. The boy grew to man's estate, the hole shrank, and there were even times when he was hard put to it to make the second shot with a 5-iron stop on the green.

Alas, however, there comes to all of us in golf the point of no return. The Ouse grows less and less Great and the poplar trees grow shorter, but the course grows longer and longer. Can this portly figure, panting flat-footedly in front of its ridiculous, if indispensable, trolley and reaching automatically for a wooden club for its second, be really the same individual playing on the same course? ' 'Tis little joy,' as the poet went on, 'to know I'm farther off from heaven than when I was a boy.'

However, there are compensations. The flat expanse on which Bedfordians play their golf can hardly be described as 'set in a sylvan setting'—as the Governor of the Darfur province of the Sudan once claimed in my presence of a hole stuck in a particularly revolting patch of camel thorn—but at least it is now liberally bestrewn with trees, and it gives one a comfortable feeling of seniority to be able to recall the time when they were planted, and to date back to the famous occasion when some short-sighted players were seen waiting on the 2nd tee under the impression that the new spinney on the right was a fourball and caddies looking for a ball.

It is something, too, to have added a word to the golfing vocabulary. As you can hook out of bounds on this course not only into the Great Ouse, but also into British Railways (Midland Region), the allotments, Mr. R.'s garden, and two fields of brussels sprouts, the youthful player develops a high precautionary slice which eats into his game and lasts a lifetime. It is a stroke which is now known to a not undistinguished circle of golfers, including Henry Cotton, as 'having a bit of Bedfordshire on it'. A poor thing, indeed, but at least mine own.

Fellow Traveller

Those who live on the route from St. Pancras to Sheffield will forgive me, I am sure, if I observe that it is not, on a grey November afternoon, the most inspiring journey in the world. The presence of the station-master, a number of inconspicuously burly gentlemen in bowler hats, and a polite crowd at the barrier was at first encouraging, but from the way your correspondent remained incognito it was only too clear that they were waiting for a superior fare. This turned out to be none other than Princess Margaret, who in a vintage saloon carriage of the old Midland Railway era, came with us as far as Chesterfield.

For me, however, the journey passed as though in a dream, for I had as my companion one who in his heyday was surely one of the most entertaining fellow-travellers in the world—Walter Hagen. Not, I need hardly say, the great man in person but the story of his life, which he has sent me from the United States.

This represents some five or six years of work on the part of as many authors, who were driven successively into frenzies of frustration by Hagen's idea of work, till only a woman, Margaret Seaton Heck, survived. 'To the Haig,' she says, 'there are no intruders on his time—only welcome interruptions'—a sentiment which may endear him to authors in the same way that his other failings, on and off the course, endeared him for twenty years to golfers.

People love to see other people spending money with a lavishness with which they know they would never have the nerve to spend it themselves, even if they had it to spend. Despite the huge fortunes run up by professional golfers in the States today, Walter Hagen probably made, and certainly spent, as much as any of them. His eight trips to the British Open, which he won four times, cost him $10,000 apiece. No wonder he twice passed the first prize straight on to his caddie!

'I travelled first class,' he says, 'and that included hotel suite at £5 a day, the Café de Paris, cocktail hour at the Ritz, the Daimler car with chauffeur and footman, planes chartered for shooting and fishing trips in northern Scotland, and parties at the Savoy Hotel, where the service was so wonderful.'

The cascade of dollars involved in living in this style for 365 days a year flowed partly from his own unsurpassed golf, partly from a four-year contract at $30,000 a year in a golf course and real estate development in Florida and partly from his meeting in the middle 'twenties a splendid character by the name of Jesse Livermore, the 'Wolf of Wall Street'.

Livermore used to sit beside four telephones, while Walter sat beside him with a fifth.

'I have two simple rules for you,' said the Wolf. 'Buy when I buy, sell when I sell,' and 'Never let a day end with one single share of stock unsold.' When the crash came and Livermore was broke and people were going down with ulcers and jumping out of windows, Walter was the more delighted that he had spent it all as it came along. 'I never wanted to be a millionaire,' he often says, 'I only wanted to live like one.'

One of my last memories of him in this country is of his arrival at Porthcawl in 1933, and he certainly looked like one then. He was sitting in the back of a vast limousine smoking a cigar with his feet up on a cabin trunk. In front beside the driver sat 'junior', a chip of the old block if ever there was one. In the tournament Hagen twice took 81, but no one wanted to watch anyone else. The party returned via Paris in the s.s. *Manhattan*, Hagen hiring the ship's orchestra for an 'all-night stand' while the vessel lay becalmed off the Statue of Liberty. Junior in the meantime had won just enough at deck games to tip the stewards, but not quite enough to pay the taxi to the hotel.

Shot Machines

A friend of mine has just been able to render to an Assistant Commissioner of the Royal Canadian Mounted Police in Manitoba a service which will warm the hearts of golfers who date back to the 'twenties, and will doubtless seem inexplicably old-fashioned to those who don't. Some thirty years ago the Assistant Commissioner, whom I like to imagine in those days as a handsome dashing figure with red tunic and prancing steed, acquired a set of irons marked with the now almost incomprehensible names of cleek, midiron, mashie, mashie-niblick and niblick.

The mashie and the niblick, it seems, were lost. Was it conceivable, he asked—in flawless copperplate handwriting as rare today as the clubs about which he was writing—that such antiquated implements were still made and that he might yet find replacements? He enclosed a drawing of the inscription on the back of the clubs, revealing them to be 'Special hand forged. Made in Scotland. T. Stewart, maker, St. Andrews.'

He also sketched in the familiar trade mark of the smoker's pipe. As a result the missing clubs, specially shafted with hickory, should now be on their way across the Atlantic, and the delighted Commissioner writes, 'That, of course, is the beauty of the fine old British institutions—how solid and permanent they are, to be sure.' It is true that closer inspection of some of the said institutions might at the moment reveal a different pattern, but it is comforting that they still seem solid and permanent when viewed from Manitoba.

Perhaps it is a sign of advancing years to compare the past favourably with the present, but in this instance I remain firmly unconvinced that golf is a more amusing game with the modern battery of clubs than it was in the days of hand-picked sets of hickory. That it was more skilful in those days would be denied, I imagine, by no one familiar with both. With his original letter the Commissioner enclosed also a sideways-on sketch of his clubs which showed them to have a sharp cutting edge instead of the flatter sole which makes the game so much less difficult today. Anyone who remembers the first steel-shafted clubs issued under Bobby Jones's imprint—the ones with the yellow shaft—will know exactly what I mean. You had only to touch the ground, especially with the niblick, for the club to bite into the turf or the sand, and the ball with a feeble sort of 'pouff' moved forward about ten feet.

Heaven forbid that I should go on record as saying that the modern broad-soled wedge has eliminated this ignominious 'fluff' from the game, but it must have reduced it by 80 per cent. Significantly, Tommy Armour declares that the wedge is almost alone responsible for the lowering of golf scores from thirty years ago. Even so, there are times when one's faith can be sorely tried, and I remember as though it were yesterday the moment before the war when, just after having written in this strain about the sand-iron, as it was then called, I found myself acting as very junior partner to Cotton in an exhibition match. Ringed with spectators, I was preparing in dead silence to play out of a bunker when a man observed, 'That's the one he says you can't miss with.'

In support of my theory I should add that, by bashing illiterately into the sand four inches behind the ball, I got it out on to the green. With a sharp-soled niblick the shot would in such circumstances have been virtually unplayable.

Perhaps the clearest circumstantial evidence of the skill exhibited by the masters of a generation ago hangs on the wall at Royal Lytham and St. Annes—the mashie-iron, also of the 'pipe' brand, with which Bobby Jones hit his championship-winning shot from bunker to green at the seventeenth thirty years ago, the carry being upwards of 170 yards. Take it down and waggle it, as anyone is at liberty to do,[1] and you find a thin, reed-like little affair by comparison with what even the most modern performer carries in his bag today—the sort of thing you would expect to pick up in a lost property office to start your fifteen-year-old daughter off with. With clubs like this Jones not only won the Open but qualified at Sunningdale with 68 and 66. Let the standardized stroke producers of today, the shot machines of modern golf, ponder on that one.

[1] Alas, no longer. It is now chained to the wall.

Trouble at Home Too

The more I see of golf the more it reminds me of life—or rather, the more I see of life the more it reminds me of golf. One moment you are three up, the birds are singing, the course has never been in more splendid order, and it is a delight indeed to be associated with a game that brings you into contact with people of such exceptional charm as your present opponent.

Half an hour later you are three down with four to play, the sun has gone in, the din set up by these damnable birds is enough to drive a man to drink, the course is in abominable condition, and life is short enough anyway without having to spend three hours of it in voluntary association with one quite so insufferable as your present opponent.

As with golf, so with life. Only the other day—how many years ago it seems now!—everything in the garden was rosy. It even seemed that in February, when our lane became blocked with snow, we might, with a little elementary plotting, shed crocodile tears for the hardships of those left at home and, instead of reporting for the intended fortnight's cure on orange juice, depart for a trip round the golf courses and other installations of Cairo, Suez, Abadan and Baghdad, returning in nice time for the University match at Sandwich.

And look at the conquering hero now, a harassed figure brooding sourly upon Nasser and all his works. The tempest

49

bellows and roars round the windmills, the rain lashes at the window panes. The patent night-and-day oil apparatus recently installed at such cost has gone out because we have run out of oil.

A moment ago, hideous caterwauling indicated that the two cats were fighting again, and, on our rushing out to separate them, one jumped for safety via the newly iced Christmas cake, a fact as yet undetected by the management.

From time to time, as someone opens the outside door, a cloud of feathers blows in from where the veteran pheasant-plucker is at work in the yard, and as a further aid to concentration there is the steady knock-knock from the adjacent downstairs bedroom broken intermittently by another wheel-barrow-load of brick rubble cascading in from the garden.

The last named is due to the recent activity *merulius lacry-mans*—aptly named, for it is enough to make anyone weep—known to the layman as dry rot or in Biblical days more picturesquely (see Leviticus XIV) as 'Leprosy of the House'. Having mentioned some weeks ago the incident of the bed falling through the bedroom floor, this particular leper has been grateful for the widespread expression of sympathy, written and oral, even though so many were facetious and some of them frankly rude.

It is a subject on which, like socketing, lumbago and gout, everyone is prepared to give expert advice or to recommend the name of a man who cured a friend of theirs, but really there is nothing you can tell me now about *mycelium*, *hyphae* or *sporophores*, which, says the pamphlet by one of the greatest living experts—and how right he is!—'soon blossom into a fleshy pancake, at first pale grey with tinges of lilac, but turning a bright rusty red as the spores are formed. . . .'

'Opening up to investigate the extent of the rot is a heart-breaking business,' he goes on, 'and requires the ruthless out-look of a successful general.' Judging by the way in which they have turned this place upside down, every one of the men he sent here has a field-marshal's baton in his knapsack. These are the men they ought to have had in the Middle

East. They would not have stopped short at Port Said. They would have been through to Karachi by now.

Still, in a moment I shall have consolation, I shall descend and walk slowly along the village street and, one after the other, people will come up and say, 'Doesn't it blow up there in the winter?' And to each I shall reply, 'Yes it does. That's why they put the —— windmills there. Ha!' And pass on.

And what has all this to do with golf? Nothing—but it reminds me of a poignant little golfing scene as a much married American Walker Cup golfer gazed at his ball lying deep in a divot mark at St. Andrews. 'Yes,' he said slowly, 'and I have trouble at home too.'

Congenital Slice

We have served out our self-imposed fourteen-day sentence and, having earned the full remission for good behaviour, will be issued with our civilian suit and released in the morning. It has been, as always, an interesting and beneficial experience. Like any other delicate piece of machinery the human body has from time to time to go in for repairs and what the soldiers always called 'maintainance', and this for the past fortnight is what we have been doing.

The rations have been meagre in the extreme—an orange for breakfast, tomato juice for lunch, tea for tea, and a cup of soup for dinner, which is 'on', roughly speaking, at 6.59 and off at 7.0. No alcohol, of course, but to a near-teetotaller like myself this is of little account—though I confess to a suspicion that, having so often walked past it with pious and averted eye during the morning exercise, I shall not readily pass by the White Hart at Witley during opening hours again.

One of the objects of this curious business, though by no means the only one, is the melting of our too, too solid flesh and those who go through life admitting cheerfully that they are 'a stone or two on the heavy side' may care to reflect that a stone represents, within an ounce or two, a full set of fourteen golf clubs. Touching on this at Rye the other day with a stout and rubicund friend, I shook him, I like to think, by observing that he was caddying permanently for half the British Walker Cup team.

At any rate, mounting the scales is an essential item of the daily routine and great are the sacrifices, not least in dignity, that we make to ensure a favourable reading. We even sit, in corpulent rows, in little 'sitz baths' of hot water with our feet in a bowl of cold, each watching his own little clock for the dread moment when it 'pings' to tell him to go and sit in the cold one with his feet in a bowl of hot. Still, it has its rewards, and I shall not lightly forget the jubilation of the noble naked lord who, on the sixth day, declared that he had 'lost all the irons and two of the woods'.

Smoking is frowned upon, and addicts are herded together to puff furtively in a communal cell. I mention it only in order to pass on a simple, perhaps rather childish but remarkably effective way of cutting one's smoking by half at a cost of twopence. When the cigarette is half-way through—which is all you want at a time anyway—you lay the lighted end on a penny. You then lay another penny gently on the top. Within seconds the cigarette goes out—don't ask me why— and may be re-lit later tasting exactly as good as before. With this I have been able to keep easily within the daily quota of ten, except for one day when at the local cinema James Mason's thriller *The Man Between*, combined with a Hollywood film so moronic as to defy description, cost me the whole of the unexpired portion of the day's ration, and I had to open another packet.

From time to time, with trousers supported by the new Woolworth braces since they will no longer keep up by themselves, our morning walk takes us as far as the West Surrey golf club and I cast my mind nostalgically back to the days when I would cheerfully bicycle five miles each way from Charterhouse, perched on a huge machine more fit for a village constable and carrying the clubs across my shoulder, and especially to that supreme triumph when the coal truck to which I had attached myself in Godalming not only turned off the Portsmouth road at Milford but actually delivered its coals to the club-house.

Though golf has been forgotten, the past fortnight may have had, for me, a profound golfing significance. On alternate days we go to have our necks ricked and such like—'never broken one yet'—by the osteopath. The other day, lying on the slab, I presented so interesting a phenomenon that he called his colleague from the adjacent cubicle to come and look. They peered learnedly together at I knew not what. No doubt about it, apparently. Yes, yes, of course. You could see it without even measuring. Right leg shorter than the left.

No wonder I have had a slice all my life! Now I know. Dammit, I was born with it!

Gezira! What memories it conjures up! The golf, the squash, the racecourse, the rugger and cricket going on side by side, the swimming pool, the reminiscences in the bar, and that ubiquitous scavenger of the East—properly, though I am afraid rarely, known as the kite—swooping down to snatch your dinner from the waiter's tray as he carried it across from the kitchen. Now Gezira is gone and 'The Doc' is no more. How much, in their different ways, they did for Egypt!

Caddies, Clerics and Cows

Of the infinite variety of relationships which we enjoy, or endure, with our fellow human beings, few have given me more pleasure than that of golfer and caddie. Perhaps it is because I got off on the right foot with the first caddie I ever had—in a children's competition at North Foreland. He was little older than I, and when he admired my white shoes I said I would give them to him if we won—and we did, and I did. After that, there passed through my memory a rich assortment of characters who have helped or hindered me round the golf course.

Some have been almost infants. In Hong Kong one is liable to be accompanied by so many that it is more like taking the kindergarten out for a walk than playing a round of golf. Others have been small boys in Middle East nightshirts; prisoners from the local gaol; American coloured men who won't go out unless they carry two bags; law students paying for their holidays; Continental girls of distracting beauty, and for good measure old Mr. Corstorphine, who carried for me in the medal at St. Andrews when he was eighty-one.

The subject arises because there has come to me a document which for its naïve simplicity and sincerity seems to me to convey this golfer-and-caddie relationship at its most delightful. It runs to thirty-five pages in a school exercise book, written in a flawless hand and, if I may say so, flawless spelling, punctuation and grammar, and consists of the reminiscences of Abe Mitchell's aunt.

Mrs. M. Mitchell is a member of one of the numerous Mitchell families so long associated with Royal Ashdown Forest, who, when they have not been caddying or working on the course, have been lending distinction to one of the best known of the artisan clubs, the Cantelupe.

Aunt Polly, as I understand her to be called, started caddying at Ashdown the best part of forty years ago, in days when she had to leave her infant son to be looked after in Jack Rowe's shop.

To the royal 'we' and the editorial 'we' should, of course, be added the 'we' of any worthwhile caddie who, since the game began, has considered his or her interests and the golfer's to be one. Mrs. Mitchell talks throughout of 'we' and it is part of her charm that the only time she says 'I' is in recounting how she was caddying one foggy wartime Sunday morning for Lord Kilbracken and could not follow the ball at all. 'I lost five balls,' she said, 'including three new ones, which I begged him not to play with.'

On making sure that his lordship was staying to lunch, she went home and put her husband's dinner ready. 'Then I put some biscuits in my pocket and took out Patsy and Judy, my two spaniels . . . and, though it was dripping with water on the trees and bracken, the dogs found all five balls. That was one occasion when I did not mind missing my Sunday dinner, although it was wartime and food was scarce.'

She remembers the names of all her golfers and their idiosyncrasies—the dawdlers, the hurriers, the under-tippers, the fidgeters, the Indian Army colonel who complained that caddies never let him get such bad lies in India. Some were distinguished visitors, like Joyce Wethered or the late Dr. A. F. Winnington-Ingram, Bishop of London, who played a young clergyman on a scorching hot day and 'felt the heat very much—he was dressed in tweeds'; or A. A. Milne, or Richard Murdoch, who arrived with a fine new cabin trunk bag one day, including shoes, haberdashery and so forth, which she emptied out at lunch-time; or the Earl of Castle Stewart, who had just bought some waterproof trousers and could not hit a shot for love nor money till she plucked up courage and said, 'Will you please forgive me, my lord, if I tell you something? I have just found out what the trouble is. You have got your trousers on the wrong way round'.

Ashdown being on common land, Mrs. Mitchell and her clients shared their golf with the birds and beasts of the common, stopping sometimes to pick up a duck's egg beside the green and hide it in the ditch against dinner-time, sometimes to remove a sleeping lamb from the line of the putt or make a calf spit out their ball, sometimes for the more dramatic business of rescuing sheep being torn to pieces by dogs in the neighbouring fields.

Then there was the singular episode of the Rev. Mr. Williams, of Copthorne, and the big red cow with the long horns. The reverend gentleman, having driven into the ditch at the seventh, picked out and dropped in a bad spot. 'He almost missed the shot and hit the cow, who was standing directly in front and swishing her tail to keep off the flies, and the ball lodged under her tail.

'The poor cow, getting more angry every minute, ran off in the direction of the green. The Rev. Williams said, "What do I do now?" I told him to drop another ball. I said, "I don't suppose the cow will go far away, so I can get your other ball." But the man on the mowing-machine, waiting to mow the fairway, was doubled up with laughter at my predicament and, of course, he was back at the golf club before I was, so they had the laugh on me.'

Mrs. Mitchell, who had to retire from regular caddying after a fall in her home some years ago, was constantly booked in advance by discerning golfers. One reason is explained when she reveals casually that, when it was too hot to wear a coat, she 'carried a tiny bag that I tied on to the golf bag, containing sponge, score-card, pencil, penknife, matches, golf tees, adhesive tape, soft rag to wipe the gloves, emery paper (before rustless clubs came into use) and a clean handkerchief'.

How interesting to compare the contents of the average caddie's pocket today!

The One and Only

By the purest coincidence I was mentioning last week that Walter Hagen's life story was due to be published in this country—without, I hoped, the trivial inaccuracies relating to golf in Britain. It is to be published tomorrow, 4 July 1960, at 30s. by Heinemann, to whom I lift my hat not only for having adjusted the inaccuracies, but also, if I may say so, for producing the pictures in much better style than in the American edition.

Every aspiring young golfer ought to be starting a golf library. He could begin by keeping a look-out for ancient copies of Sir Walter Simpson's *Art of Golf*, and the immortal Badminton volume edited by Horace Hutchinson. Thereafter he might do well to stick to people rather than mere instruction, on which subject books pour from the presses almost every day. J. H. Taylor's *Golf, My Life Work*, comes to mind. Cotton's *This Game of Golf*, *The Bobby Jones Story*, and, of course, a selection of vintage Darwin.

I think our appreciation of Hagen was mutual. He had every reason at first to dislike England. He arrived at Deal in 1922, in clothes flamboyant by our standards, as the youthful U.S. Open Champion, and, having attracted much attention, finished 53rd. Furthermore, it was in the days when professionals were not allowed in the club-house—just as caddies are not today, which I suppose will be dismissed as 'snobbery' in twenty years' time.

Hagen's comment was 'I'll be back'. He came back, and grew to appreciate the true qualities of the great seaside links and to savour the many-sided life of our small island. Everybody loved—and forgave—him, and even today, Gene Sarazen often says, on his coming to England veteran caddies will at once come up and ask, 'Ow's 'ighgen?'

Other people's comments, which serve as chapter headings for his book, will illuminate Hagen's character for those who never have the luck to share his company. That penetrating critic Arthur Croome, for instance, wrote on his first arrival, 'It was at once borne in on me that here was a man who would not fail through excess of modesty. . . He makes more bad shots during a season than Harry Vardon did during the whole period 1890–1914, in the course of which he won six open championships, but he beats more immaculate golfers because "three of those and one of them" counts four and he knows it.'

While Hogan has slaved away to perfect a swing which, as he puts it, 'repeats', Hagen had an almost amateurish style and relied on his sensitive touch—even when he had not been to bed the night before. Said Tommy Armour, 'He can gauge balls from the lightest to the heaviest, arranging them in order when there is only a pennyweight of difference between half a dozen. If the scales don't check with Walter's guess, the scales are wrong.'

Not only his bad shots and consequent recoveries endeared him to the public—he once went through a championship at Sandwich without a six, though several times bunkered in three—but also the way in which he alternated so cheerfully between affluence and insolvency.

'Hagen,' said the late Grantland Rice, 'made well over a million in golf and spent it all. Money has never meant anything to him except something to get rid of quickly. How he ever took the beating that he gave himself is beyond anyone's imagination.'

He it was, undoubtedly, who opened up the golden road which American professionals follow so much less entertainingly today. 'All of them,' says Sarazen, 'should say a silent thanks to him whenever they stretch a cheque between their fingers. It was Walter who made professional golf what it is.'

The late Bob Harlow was his long suffering manager for eleven years. 'With a broad expansive grin on his features,' he wrote, 'Hagen looks at the world through the hole in the doughnut—and keeps his hand on the dough.' Walter in return writes of Harlow, 'Through all those years we never had a written contract of any sort. He set up the dates, I played the tournaments and exhibitions, and we carried the greenbacks away in an old suitcase. It was an ideal arrangement. It allowed me to relax and enjoy my friends and my game.'

Therein perhaps lay his secret. Unlike some of the experts of today, he palpably enjoyed his golf and his life and his friends, and asked of the world only that it should come in and share the fun. The master gamesman himself, he was absolute proof against the first principle of gamesmanship, namely, to get the other man flurried and tensed up. To my friend Fred Corcoran, who was in difficulties with some tournament he was organizing, he expressed his whole philosophy of life: 'Don't worry, Fred,' he drawled, 'don't hurry. We're only here a little time. Never forget to stop and smell the flowers.'

Among my favourite biographies is *W. C. Fields: His Follies and Fortunes*. Hagen was the W. C. Fields of golf. They bore the same initials, their life stories might well have borne the same title.

Poignant Moments

Perhaps it is a sign of advancing years, but I always find it fascinating to gaze back and recapture the spirit and flavour of golf in its early days rather than to peer into what seems likely to be an increasingly costly, complicated and sophisticated future, when everyone perhaps will take as a matter of course the local rule of the club on which we played the last Ryder Cup match in California, namely that players on foot have no standing on the course. They must step aside for the motorized battalions in their electric buggies to come through!

Only the other day Lord Bruce of Melbourne was showing me a newspaper cutting which quoted from a new publication, the Australian Golfers' Handbook, the circumstances in which his father, Mr. J. M. Bruce, founded golf in Melbourne in 1890.

He had brought his family back to England for two years and on his return, says Lord Bruce, 'he took back with him a very large assortment of golf clubs—I believe it was some hundreds—and proceeded to stun all his friends into joining a golf club'. Actually he stunned eighty in two days at fifteen guineas a time.

I must pass over the official opening of the original course (4,750 yards: bogey 87: record, until 1895, 80) by Mr. Bruce and Mr. Playfair, grandson of Sir Hugh Lyon Playfair whose portrait hangs over the fireplace at the Royal and Ancient, and come to the purpose of my story, namely to recall the scene at the opening of the second Royal Melbourne at Sandringham by the Lieutenant-Governor, Sir John Madden, ten years later.

Sir John, according to a contemporary account, was a polished and distinguished speaker and his performance on this occasion constituted one of those little oratorical gems which audiences had learned to expect. When it came to driving off the first ball, however, he found himself less happily placed. He does not appear to have been endowed by nature with any great faculty for the game nor had he made any attempt to remedy by art his natural infirmities as a golfer.

'He commenced by announcing that he had "never played the game before in his life", a remark that subsequent events proved superfluous. The large and fashionable gathering was hushed as he took his stance and addressed the ball. He flourished his driver, looked up expectantly, and delivered himself of a hearty whack . . . there was an outburst of undiluted merriment in which Sir John himself joined. If his first shot did not open the links, it certainly opened the tee.'

With a restraint which may seem strange to the Australian sporting Press today, the *Melbourne Argus* reported: 'His first shot was unsuccessful, scattering the turf in various directions. The second, however, sent the ball flying some yards away.'

This compares favourably with the report, when a Very Important Captain drove himself in at St. Andrews with a shot that just missed the square-leg umpire. 'His Royal Highness hit a rather low ball, slightly to the left.' It was Sir Guy Campbell, I believe, who reported that some of the caddies waiting to retrieve the ball stood 'disloyally close to the tee'.

This solitary driving-oneself-in represents one of the most poignant single moments in a man's life. I have even in minor circumstances done it myself, the ball curving high in the air and finishing where I knew, and any of my friends will have known, that it would—behind an elm tree 200 yards away on the right. Lord Brabazon, after surreptitious practice swings in his shirtsleeves behind the St. Andrews' bandstand, hit a low 'runner' which had come to rest some time before the caddies could dash forward and retrieve it. He described it at the dinner as a 'noble gesture of self denial which has given pleasure to thousands'.

Last year Dr. Harold Gardiner-Hill, I believe, though I am afraid I overslept and was only woken by the cannon, nearly lost his opening shot altogether. It vanished in the early morning mist and was not found for some minutes. Mr. John Beck has already had three months, and has still another two, in which to contemplate his supreme moment on 18 September.[1] He may console himself with the thought that Willie Auchterlonie, who will tee his ball, is possessed of at least as much tact as the old British professional who performed this function for a corpulent German prince on opening a course on the Continent.

He missed the ball altogether. 'And now,' said the professional, so that all could hear, 'If your Royal Highness is ready, I think the opening stroke should be made.'

[1] He hit a beauty.

67

Walker Cup Jottings, 1957

After a splendid transatlantic flight in the B.O.A.C. Strato-cruiser *Canopus* and a short stop for breakfast and showers at the Royal Montreal Club, the Walker Cup golf team may be reported as being in fine fettle for the first leg of their operational schedule, the Canadian Amateur Championship.

Canopus is the aeroplane in which the Queen flew to the West Indies on her Commonwealth tour, though doubtless her private accommodation was in the first-class quarters in the tail, all of which was in our own case occupied by a party of adolescent and rather nondescript National Servicemen en route for Christmas Island, attired in anything from boots to brown slippers.

After a good deal of jollification between Prestwick, where we picked up the Scottish contingent, and Iceland, Dr. Deighton dispensed some welcome transquillizers of exceptional severity and peace reigned throughout the night, one of our married couples remaining blissfully unconscious for seven hours. Incidentally, we have three wives accompanying us and, though we may not win the Walker Cup, I would back them in a beauty-cum-charm contest against any three the Americans cared to put in the field.

The 7½-hour daylight flight from Montreal to Winnipeg at a steady tourist-class jog-trot pace passed without incident, though when the National Service adolescents flashed by in a

Viscount there were dark mutterings about clubbing together to send a cable to the Member for Brentford and Chiswick, himself a past Walker Cup captain,[1] suggesting a question to the Minister of Defence relating to further possible economies in his department.

All the same, for the newcomer, this is a wonderful flight. For five or six hundred miles one passes over unending forest and lakes uninhabited and unexplored by man, save the pioneers, who somehow drove the railway through to the West Coast and to whom I lifted my hat in retrospective respect as this morning I inspected the first Canadian Pacific locomotive, *Countess of Dufferin*, which stands, complete with cowcatcher and huge spout-like funnel, outside my hotel door.

After a few tentative holes of golf, we spent our first evening at the opening of the football season, the Winnipeg Bombers losing to the champion Edmonton Eskimos, who, with their curious padded shapes and golden helmets, looked more than ever like men from Mars.

The team were given a friendly cheer by 18,000 spectators and the warmest of welcomes by Stewart McPherson, who runs the stadium. We broadcast together after the match and he recalled how we had first performed together from the silence room of the Royal and Ancient club-house at St. Andrews during Sam Snead's Open Championship, the first to penetrate the sacred precincts for that purpose in those, shall we say, less enlightened days.

Having now played the course, I can say that it represents the best form of North Atlantic 'target golf' with wide fairways and well-watered greens, on which even the half-topped iron shot will carve out an appreciable divot and stop on the green. One wonders to what extent Henry Cotton would have murdered it in the 'thirties with every shot to the green stopping within a yard or so of its pitch. Nevertheless, many of the holes take intelligent playing, because they have left groups of trees directly in the line of play. Three of our team

[1] P. B. Lucas, D.S.O., D.F.C.

were round in 70 this morning, including Sewell, whose curious putting method to everyone's relief appears to work as well on this side of the Atlantic as the other.

Tomorrow morning while teams of four from each Canadian Province play for the Willingdon Cup, our own players will be playing for a captain's prize put up by Micklem, and I am flattered to report that, as a result of some observation of mine about past matches, they are all to have a compulsory sweepstake on the first five holes, over which so many past teams have lost in the first hour.

All of us feared that the heat might be intolerable, but so far everything has been perfect. My young caddie, Brian Eardsley (aged thirteen), assures me that all will be well. He says that his grandparents and innumerable cousins and aunts live in the Woking area. On my giving him the standard fee of just over one pound and expressing the hope that he would soon be a millionaire in this miraculously expanding country, he said: 'At this rate I certainly will be.' The British team have to qualify over 36 holes on Monday and Tuesday for sixty-four players. I see no reason why all of them at the current rate should not do so nor why one of them should not come home as Canadian Champion.[1] I find it impossible not to believe that this is potentially the best Walker Cup team we have sent across the water.

*

Among the many curious illusions under which the average citizen of the United States labours regarding our country is that it always rains in Britain, just as the non-Lancastrian is convinced that it is now, was yesterday and tomorrow will be raining in Manchester. If anyone, however, is interested in seeing it really rain let him come to Minneapolis in August. This is the real thing.

Having said which I must pay tribute to the Minikahda course. In no part of the world have I seen a golf course

[1] No luck of course!

stand up to such a downpour as we saw yesterday afternoon for the foursomes. I cannot think of a single British course, seaside or inland, that would not have been waterlogged.

Another surprise is that no one on either side took advantage of the rule allowing players to take shelter from lightning. I am not sure I should have wanted to be out in this with a battery of steel-shafted clubs.

A 2,000 crowd followed the morning play under leaden grey skies heavy with rain, though not yet releasing it, but for pretty well the whole of the second round it was like playing in a warm showerbath with the tap turned full on. I doubt whether any golfing crowd has been so thoroughly and mercilessly soaked as the small body of enthusiasts who stuck it to the end. This being in the heart of Hiawatha country it is difficult to resist comments on 'laughing water'.

*

This week has been a kind of interim stage between the second and third of the three 'tasks' which the British Walker Cup captain, Gerald Micklem, has emphasized throughout to be the objects of the present expedition, namely the Canadian Championship, the Walker Cup and the United States Championship.

Whatever the record may suggest, we certainly showed an interim dividend in the principal event last week-end.

Though naturally loath to create excuses for failing to gain what no visiting team has ever gained before, I should like to 'recap', as they say on the panel games, to the extent of reminding you that at one point we led by some margin, however small, in five out of the eight singles. Indeed there was a moment during the afternoon when, if play had ceased there and then, we should actually have won.[1]

Before leaving, I wrote that Canadian and American friends had warned me that the heat could conceivably be crippling. We saw no sign of it in either country—till the very

[1] Final result U.S.A. 8½, Britain 3½.

day of the singles, when the temperature shot to 94 in the shade with a humidity content, I am told, of 98 per cent. I shall go to my grave declaring that this single freak of weather prevented this fine British team from achieving one of the outstanding victories in golfing history. What is more, I fancy that the American captain, Charles Coe, would agree.

From Minneapolis we repaired to Pine Valley, near Philadelphia, to supplement the golfing education of those who had not played this greatest of all inland courses before. It was, as usual, a stimulating if humbling experience. This course, designed by Harry Colt in the 'nineties, is the supreme scholarship examination in golf. All the questions are perfectly fair, but to the average candidate it is like being set a long piece of Homer unseen when the best you can normally do is Xenophon with the aid of a dictionary.

The par is 70 and they will bet almost any first-time visitor that he will not beat it by 18 up in receipt of five strokes per hole. They never lose. As an old hand I fear that I held forth in the aeroplane to the effect that all you had to do was to keep the ball in play and not be intimidated by propaganda, etcetera, on the basis of which I snapped up sundry insulting offers by that inveterate wagerer, Joe Carr, about my getting round in 89. I know of no other course in the world on which even with borrowed clubs your humble servant could be two over fours for the first five holes and 27 over for the remaining thirteen—total 101.

Bonallack, with whom I had the pleasure of playing, played absolutely beautifully to share the honours with Scrutton with 76; Sewell had a 77 and Carr, I report with some relish, 83. So now, after a quick visit to Winged Foot, where many old friendships were re-established from the 1949 match, including that of the great sage, Tommy Armour, and many members of the locker-room staff, we find ourselves at one of the most senior and revered clubs in the States, the Country Club, Brookline. Incidentally, to call it the Brookline Country Club is akin to referring to the Royal and Ancient as the St. Andrews Golf Club.

Much golfing history has been made here, but nothing will

ever equal 20 September 1913, when Francis Ouimet—ex-caddie at the club, aged twenty, with seven hickory-shafted clubs in a canvas bag, carried by Ed Lowery; a little boy in a white hat destined later to become a member of the U.S.G.A. Executive Committee—not only tied with the British giants, Harry Vardon and Ted Ray, but also beat them on the play-off. Their cards, Ouimet, 72, Vardon 77, Ray 78 are in a glass case in the club-house, Ouimet's bearing the marker's signature of Bernard Darwin.

As to the championship this week, I remain incorrigibly full of hope. The myth that American amateur golfers are unbeatable has been exploded—or whatever you do to myths in order to cause them to vanish. After their oh-so-near miss at Minneapolis, not a single member of this team, especially the more juvenile, believes in it any more.

Out of an entry of 1,592, some 200 are assembled here—169 through regional qualifying, such as we ourselves are to have for the first time next year, and 31 through exemptions, which include the Walker Cup teams and captains, all past British and American champions, and the reigning American senior, junior and public links champions.

Our own championship being at the moment in a state of experimental change, perhaps the most interesting point to me is that the draw has been seeded, the two Walker Cup teams being evenly distributed down the list. This has been the making of Wimbledon, and I find more and more support for doing it in golf at home. However, never mind that.

All I ask now is that at midnight Greenwich Mean Time next Saturday I shall be telephoning over the miraculous new underwater cable, which makes you feel as though you were in the next room, as to which of the two British finalists is being acclaimed as the new American Amateur Champion. It could not happen, you say? It could, you know.[1]

[1] It couldn't, you know.

Glorious Day at Lindrick

Britain's golfers surpassed the hopes of even the wildest optimists by winning the Ryder Cup from the United States here today for the first time for twenty-four years. After starting the day 1–3 down in the foursomes they won the singles by six matches to one, with one halved, to triumph overall by $7\frac{1}{2}$–$4\frac{1}{2}$.

This must be one of the most notable days[1] in the history of international golf between Britain—or 'Great Britain and Eire' as it is now more correctly styled—and the United States.

It never really occurred to me that there was the slightest chance of getting more than three points in the two days, and when asked by interested parties before the match I cheerfully revealed to all and sundry the opinion that we 'should not win a match on either day'. This seems to be the winning formula and I propose to repeat it before all future Ryder, Walker and Curtis Cup matches.

The historic day dawned fine but rather cold. It warmed up as it went on but cooled off noticeably towards the end, as though to do all it could to chill the fingers and spirits of our distinguished adversaries, who spend most of their working lives in lush club-houses and benevolent sunshine.

[1] 5 October 1957.

74

It is, I repeat, twenty-four years since we won this Cup—or even, with one exception at Wentworth four years ago, looked like doing so—and only a few of us among the 'regulars' remember seeing Syd Easterbrook at Southport and Ainsdale holing the curly four-footer—the last stroke of the last match on the last day—that won it for Britain in 1933.

For myself, I have for some years been brooding on dark thoughts that really it was hardly worth playing again. I now lift my hat to Dai Rees and his merry men and ask leave to withdraw.

To do justice to today's play by the British team I could hardly do better than write 'Please see all previous reports of final day's play in Ryder and Walker Cup matches and for American read British'.

Flitting from match to match I saw a great many brave putts holed, and on almost every occasion it was a British player that holed them. I also saw a good many short ones missed and nearly always, unaccountably, it was our opponents.

With a stiffish breeze blowing against at the first hole and rising during the day, Lindrick, with its narrow gorse-lined fairways, was a test of nerves and skill despite its mere 6,541 yards against the 7,000-odd generally reckoned necessary for a proper test these days. And, in fact, not a single man on either side broke 70 all day. The strict professional par is about 69.

With every score at every hole in front of me I find that the British averaged about 71. The Americans soared several times into the high seventies. How this could conceivably be I still do not know—and I know, from talking to them, that they don't either.

From the word go it was Britain's day. They all shot out of the trap to early leads—as the Americans had done on Friday—and bravely they held on to them. For the first fifty holes played they were eleven under fours, the Americans eight over.

Perhaps the two heroes were Brown and Rees, the latter

winning his vital foursome and playing another captain's innings today; the former matching himself in a no-love-lost game with the most combative character in American golf today.

Round in 71, Brown was four up on Bolt at lunch. He was reduced to two, holed a vital putt to win the seventh, was reduced to two again but never wavered to win by 4 and 3, and draw first blood for Britain.

Bolt, who is distinguished for club-throwing in America, actually went so far at the last hole of the match as to bang his club into the ground and break it.

He was followed by Mills, a frail figure beside the American captain, Burke, who had left himself out of the singles and came in at the last moment for Kroll, who was sick. No one could see Mills winning this on form, but away he went with a 71 against 77 to be 5 up and he, too, never looked like faltering.

Alliss, the only one to lose, can look back with satisfaction on a score of one under fours for the day and on drawing the only man, Fred Hawkins, who played like the old-time American.

Bousfield, 71 against 76, never looked like being challenged —and so it went on. It is no reflection on the British team to say that those of us who have seen so many of these matches were looking to see where the crack was coming. It never came. Not a man faltered. Every few minutes tremendous cheers arose from all quarters of the course to signify a British win. Our American friends must not think us too partial. We don't often see these things.

In the fifth match came Rees, four under fours for 17 holes—he picked up at the other—four up on Furgol. In the afternoon level fours for 12 holes, he forged on to win by 7 and 6.

Hunt, approximately 71, was one up on Ford, possibly the best short-game player in America. Out in 33 he went on to win by 6 and 5.

Then we came to O'Connor, the match-play champion, all square with a 71 against the coming American 'hope',

Finsterwald. He went off after lunch with 4, 4, 3, 4, 4, 3, 4, 3, picked up at the ninth, went on with a two, and was home and dry by 7 and 6.

So, one by one, the Americans of all people had collapsed and only Mayer, the Open Champion, was left. He was one up at lunch but Bradshaw's 71 earned him a half—of academic interest only, now, but how valuable it might have been.

Well, there is is. We have lived to see the day again. What happened to the Americans I do not know, but I look forward for once to seeing articles headed 'What is wrong with American golf?' I suspect somehow that our adversaries did not wholly enjoy their stay, but nothing can take away the glory from Rees and his team. I still can't quite believe it, but it will be for ever in the book of records that at Lindrick we beat the flower of American professional golf by seven matches to four with one halved.

*

At the finish of the Ryder Cup match, which did indeed warrant the overworked word 'sensational', I could neither believe it nor account for it. I can believe it now, but I still cannot account for it.

One thing, however, stands out a mile, namely that, while one or two bits of extraneous unpleasantness may have momentarily taken some of the gilt off his gingerbread, Dai Rees deserves a pat on the back from every follower of sport in Britain and for that matter in Eire, which though 'under entirely new management' in other directions, is still for golfing purposes incorporated with the old firm.

Rees's personal contribution to this astonishing victory was as great as any I can remember in any team match, be it international, University, Halford Hewitt, or anything else. In the foursomes he and Bousfield were two down during the morning, all square at lunch, and two down again with eleven to play. By this time we knew that only a win from them could avoid a clean sweep. If there was to be the faintest chance on the morrow, they must get home somehow—and they did.

In the singles his score, apart from one hole where he picked up, was the best on either side, but above all his personal zest and enthusiasm kept up the spirits of a side which, 3–1 down at the end of the first day, was looking almost certain defeat in the eye.

Canada Cup in Tokyo

Japan, represented by Torakichi Nakamura, their forty-two-year-old champion, and Koichi Ono, are in an almost unassailable position in the Canada Cup[1] international tournament here. After 54 holes they lead the field by nine strokes from Snead and Demaret, of the United States, with South Africa and Wales tying for third place, and in the individual tournament Nakamura is out on his own at 203, seven shots ahead of David Thomas, of Wales.

The world, they say, is a small place, to which I can only reply that a vast amount of it seems to lie between Alberta and Japan. The first stage was accomplished via Canadian Pacific Railway's amazing line through the Rockies, where it twice turns upon itself inside the mountain in a complete mile-long circle, re-emerging just below where it went in. This brought us to the fair city of Vancouver, where kind friends took me to lunch at the celebrated Capilano Club. Looking down over the harbour and across to Victoria, it did not take long to appreciate why so many English people choose to end their days in retirement there, and I almost made a resolution to join them.

The next stop by contrast was an aptly named refuelling strip on the tip of Alaska called Cold Bay, where the most

[1] November 1957.

79

animated of fifty-odd inhabitants is undoubtedly a black retriever, who meets every visiting aeroplane, wagging an anticipatory tail at the bottom of the steps. On this occasion he completed at midnight a record day—retrieving 7 geese, 12 duck, 21 ptarmigan and a large steak from one of the air hostesses.

After thirteen more hours' non-stop flying, illuminated towards the end by an unidentified volcano in eruption below, we saw Mount Fuji suspended in the dawn sky and knew that we were nearly home.

From all quarters of the globe representatives of no fewer than thirty nations, including among them China, Chile, Korea, Columbia and Siam had been converging for what has been described, not unreasonably, as the greatest international sporting event ever held in the Far East. Some of them had been flying continuously for four days.

The scene of this year's Canada Cup contest, the Kasumigaseki Country Club, is reached after nearly two hours' combined hooting and driving, the hazards of the journey being only partly alleviated by the fact that they do at least drive on the right side of the road, namely the left.

The golf course, judged by highest European or American standards, is unusually good, and I remember none to which more sincere or spontaneous tributes have been paid. It resembles, perhaps, the new course at Sunningdale, with every hole lined by fir trees, or, for Scottish readers, a 6,900 yard edition of Blairgowrie. Its condition is reflected by the fact that 250 women and girls have for some months been going over it on hands and knees removing the slightest blemish.

The cream of these have been selected as caddies and are attired in a uniform of blue peaked cap, red jacket embroidered with their player's name and country, blue trousers and white shoes. All are trim as tulips, and many would fit easily into the enormous golf bags they so cheerfully shoulder.

Snead set a cracking pace with 67, supported by an admirable 69 from Demaret, who for some years has remained aged forty-seven, and together they led the field, with Japan second, Wales and England trailing 10 shots behind, Ireland 12 and Scotland 14.

It is a further tribute to the course that on this lovely autumn day only seven players beat the par of 72. Yesterday Nakamura with another fine 68 put Japan into a two-shot lead over the United States, while Thomas with a 67 brought Wales to fifth place.

In the individual championship he, Peter Alliss, Peter Thomson and Demaret shared second place to Nakamura with 140, Snead dropping back with 74. Thomas's partner, Dai Rees, declared his round to be the most perfect he had ever seen. It might honestly have been 62 he said.

Today, under lowering skies, we have seen some truly extraordinary golf and an exhibition of the short game by Nakamura and Ono that left their fellow-competitors, Player and Henning, of South Africa, open-eyed with wonder.

Nakamura, short and wiry, has a two-piece backswing and a good deal of sway, and will take two wooden club shots where Alliss needs only a drive and a 5-iron, but when he gets to the green Nakamura is more like a conjurer than a golfer. Ono, a slim Manchurian who came over as a caddie years ago, is more orthodox, but equally deadly. Between them they had only 53 putts.

Nakamura, with 68, 68, 67, stands away out on his own and the pair of them, with a total of 414 and one round to play, do not seem even remotely likely to be caught.[1]

Of our own contingent, Wales alone have held their place and lie third, fourteen shots behind, Thomas again having distinguished himself with a 70. For England, Alliss had three bad holes and he and Bousfield lie seventh with 434, while Scotland are eleventh at 449, three strokes behind the Philippine Islands and 35 behind Japan—enough to make old Tom Morris either turn in his grave or reflect with

[1] They were not. Japan won the Canada Cup with ease from the United States and Nakamura defeated Snead for the individual trophy by no fewer than seven shots.

wonder that the elementary game he knew should thus have spread to the farthest corners of the earth. For Ireland, Harry Bradshaw, having already been 'hospitalized' for persistent nose-bleeding, had unhappily to retire.

So now the stage is set for two Japanese wins tomorrow in what may fairly be called the Olympic Games of golf. Judging by the enthusiasm shown to date, it would not surprise me if we had 20,000 people out here to see them do it. The whole thing is an experience I would not have missed for worlds. If the British win the Ryder Cup and the Japanese win the Canada Cup, where do we go next?

*

My only previous acquaintance with that country being made through a travelogue film—'And so farewell to the land of slant-eyed women and the rising sun, Japan'—I have now left it with much regret. There are aspects of life in Japan which the Westerner may both respect and envy though, since most of them bear no possible relation to golf, it is not within my province to hold forth upon them here.

As I sit in the darkened aeroplane somewhere between Tokyo and Alaska, surrounded by itinerant Chinese and a posse of comatose South American golf professionals who are destined to sit, sleep and eat in the same narrow chair for four whole days before they reach their homes, I fall continuously to reflecting what a wonderful game is golf in taking us all over the world in this fashion.

Next door to me, looking leaner than ever, there sleeps Mario Gonzales, a great lover of English life whom many will remember as a semi-finalist in the 1948 Amateur Championship at Sandwich when he was beaten by Stranahan. In Tokyo I said good-bye to Rees, Bousfield, Bradshaw and O'Connor. They were setting off the other way round the world, playing their way home with exhibition matches at Hong Kong, Singapore and, I believe, Bangkok.

A day or two previously Alliss, Thomas, Panton, Brown and the two South Africans, Player and Henning, had flown to play in five events in Australia. This will be a fine experience for all of them, not least for Thomas, in whom we have beyond question the rising star of British golf.

Wherever the Canada Cup may go in the future, it will have no keener reception than in Japan, where the game is surging through the country, as it did through the United States after Harry Vardon's tours at the turn of the century. At the nine-hole course where the winner, Nakamura, is professional, people book in before dawn, wait three hours, play nine holes, book in again, wait another three hours, which they spend mostly on the practice range, and then play another nine.[1]

At the other end of the scale are resorts like Kawana, where I spent my last day. The magnificent hotel, again reminiscent of Turnberry, looks down on the sea and on two fine golf courses which wind their way between tangerine groves and those slanting beachside fir trees with which we in England are familiar through Japanese prints.

Nevertheless, my principal memory remains not of the beauties of nature, but of the artificial adornment of man. Like Bing Crosby, the redoubtable Sam Snead at forty-five is somewhat thin on top. 'Will ah go put mah rug on?' he said, as we prepared one evening for a party at the Canadian Embassy.

Encouraged by all, he disappeared and returned five minutes later transformed into the early 'thirties. His 'rug' proved to be positively the finest wig ever seen. They say it cost him $125. They also say he got it second-hand. Alas, however, for the vanity of man. Snead in his natural state stands out anywhere as a man of distinction. Adorned with his rug he vanished in the crowd.

[1] Since this time the rise in popularity of golf in Japan has been fantastic and the game has even become something of a status symbol. Several hundred driving ranges have sprung up, one with three storeys, others in nets on top of the main buildings.

Happy Homecoming

As we boarded the aeroplane last week-end our clothes were sticking to us, and even the inhabitants of Boston were complaining of the heat and humidity. As we stepped out at Prestwick, the same clothes were instantly unstuck by the perishing early morning blast and even the inhabitants of Scotland were complaining of the cold. For myself I survived the journey to St. Andrews, but thereafter proved a pushover for every germ in the vicinity—whether Asian or Scotch I do not know—and the past week has consequently been one of enforced contemplation.

The principal items in life, instead of the autumn meeting, the Medal, and the Masters Tournament, have been the strepto-something or other mixture to combat the germs; the pink anti-wheeze mixture, reminiscent of the 'grenadine' we used to get from the school tuckshop, with a touch of vodka added; the anaesthetic lozenges not to be chewed or swallowed; and the brown bomb-like pills designed to combat any unfortunate effects of the white mixture.

It strikes me that this may be the result of having been linked with Douglas Bader for the Medal. His first partner-designate, Lord Brabazon, had a heart attack. The second, myself, was knocked out immediately on arrival. The third, an American, actually reached the tee, but, having read perhaps that we liked to play rather faster in this country, had so adjusted his arrangements that he had to walk in from the thirteenth in order to catch a train for Paris.

However, from my bed of sickness I heard the cannon go off to signify that John Beck had driven himself in as captain, and kind friends came in to tell me not only of his splendid stroke, the best for thirty years, but also of the singular episode of Mr. Henry Turcan and the Knight on the Shooting Stick. This occurred among the customary hold-up on the 2nd tee and deserves, I think, a wider public.

Mr. Turcan, as sometimes happens, had struck his second to the first hole on to the ladies' putting course away to the right—a safe if unambitious stroke, which left him a simple pitch to the green. A way having been made for him through the players and caddies waiting on the 2nd tee and the crowd which had gathered there to watch the 'Legless Wonder',[1] he played an admirable shot—only to have it smartly fielded, first bounce, by the Knight on the Shooting Stick and hurled back.

On interrogation the Knight averred that he was under the impression that Mr. Turcan was practising. At any rate, his return throw was such as to leave the player now faced with a carry of ten or twelve yards over the Swilcan Burn, and this, understandably in the circumstances, he failed to make. However, one is not a member of the Rules of Golf Committee for nothing, and even as he was duffing the ball into the burn, Mr. Turcan was calculating that he ought really to be replacing it, free of charge, at the spot where the Knight had fielded it. This he proceeded to do—and thereupon chipped it up stone dead for one of the most curious fives in golfing history.

[1] Group Captain Douglas Bader, D.S.O., D.F.C., who lost his legs in an air crash in 1922 and plays to a handicap of 9.

Game Within a Game

The art of putting at golf resembles that of goalkeeping at soccer, in being 'a game within a game'. Furthermore, as I remember so often reflecting as I leant nonchalantly against the uprights—having played in goal since the age of eight—both are games which enable a fellow with a certain crafty cunning to neutralize the efforts of stronger, braver men, and this in any walk of life is a source of much inward satisfaction.

An exception perhaps was when I kept goal for a year behind an accomplished cricketer, who is now a housemaster at Charterhouse. It will not, I hope, lead to insubordination in the *alma mater* if I reveal that, playing at right back, he scored for every one of the eleven houses in the school—including, on an historic occasion, our own.

On the other hand, both putting and goalkeeping may lead to an embarrassing immortality not to be endured in other departments of the game. The poor wretch who lets it trickle slowly between his legs in a Cup Final is remembered long after missers of sitting goals have sunk into a merciful oblivion. A yard putt missed on the last green may also live for ever.

Thoughts of putting come to my mind because I have recently mentioned the four secrets of putting, as outlined to me one day years ago by Bobby Locke, who was presumably the greatest holer-out in the world in the post-war years, and one or two peole have asked to be let in upon them.

I hope that I am not poaching on Locke's professional pre-serves in revealing them. A good agent, I should have said, could have got him £1,000 for them.

ONE: You must hit the ball clean. This does not involve any nonsense about 'top spin' or 'trying to make it roll'. If you flick a ping-pong ball off a table, you take aim with your finger-nail and flick it cleanly. Touch the table and you 'smudge' it. It is the same with brushing the putter along the grass.

'You can tell a good putt,' says Locke, 'by the noise it makes'—and very remarkable it is to hear him demonstrate, interspersing clean hits with an odd one just touching the grass. Ping, ping, PUNG, ping, ping, PUNG, they go—and so on. It occurs to me that Locke was probably the loudest putter in golf.

TWO: Every putt you will ever have in your life, on any course, in any country, of any length, is dead straight. Ele-mentary, when you come to think of it—but had you thought of it that way? Of course, on a sharp slope the ball may roll almost in a semi-circle—but you did not make it do so. All you can do, time and time and time again, is to hit it dead straight—not necessarily, of course, straight at the hole. A bullet fired in a high wind at Bisley will travel in a slight curve. The man who gets a bull with it adjusted his sights and aimed straight. The mental relief on grasping this simple conception is unbelievable.

THREE: Hold the putter very loosely. 'Ha!' I remember saying, 'and what about when you have a four-footer to tie for the Open?' 'Hold it looser still!' he said. Touching wood, in a good hour be it spoken and all the rest of it, I do verily believe this may be at least partially the cure for the 'jitters'. Sufferers might perhaps report later.[1]

---

[1] I really think there may be something in this. Like many other moderate golfers who play in the spring and autumn meetings of the Royal and Ancient though without the least hope of winning so much as a handicap prize, I am afflicted acutely with the 'twitch' on these occasions. Last time, by holding the club so loosely that it almost fell out of my hands, I got the whole way round without a single twitch.

FOUR: Any fool can putt through a hoop four feet wide from ten yards or more. In other words, you take three putts through getting the distance wrong, not the direction. So when Locke wanders slowly between ball and hole, he is not, as one might suppose, pondering on the infinite or looking for leather-jackets. He is making up his mind how far it is. See also Rule One.

If you sometimes hit it clean and sometimes touch the grass, it may make a difference of four or five feet in distance —the difference between two putts and three.

FIVE: This is my own, based merely on observation. Locke evolved a 'drill'. Never mind the details—we can all evolve our own. In other words, for every putt he ever made, irrespective of distance or circumstances, once the machinery was set in action he went through the same motions. No extra waggle, no extra look at the hole. For better or for worse. Which is yet another reason, I fancy, why it was almost inevitably for better.

Back to Work

After hopping in and out of innumerable aeroplanes and being carried therein a distance equal almost to the orbit of a flying dog, it has been a great delight to get one's feet firmly on the ground again and to enjoy a game of golf at St. Andrews. We were able after a steaming rainstorm at midday—real Somerset Maugham stuff—to complete our eighteen holes in shirtsleeves and sunshine and to finish the evening on the terrace gazing out over our whiskies and soda at the fireflies dancing in the darkness and the lights of the ships at anchor in the bay.

Lest any of my friends at the Home of Golf should fancy that I had begun to 'see things', I should explain that the St. Andrews in question is in Port of Spain and is the senior golf club in Trinidad. Later I was able to pay a visit even nearer home as it seemed, to the Brighton Club—without the 'and Hove'—and to note, with due respect to the Sussex edition, of which I have the honour to be a member, that I would rather play my winter golf there among the palm trees, looking down over gentle slopes to the dazzling blue Gulf of Paria and the distant islands, than in a howling gale on the Downs looking down over the Shoreham power station.

The journey to Brighton, which lies hard beside the celebrated Trinidad asphalt lake—a rather dreary natural phenomenon 'worth seeing', as Dr. Johnson remarked of the Giant's Causeway, 'but not worth going to see'—involved a long drive down through the sugar plantations and a stop to drop off a member of the party who was playing Rugby football against British Guiana on the ground of the Trinidad Leaseholds Company, over whose sale to the Texans there had been a good deal of recent fuss. Next door, such is the climate of this lovely island, there was a cricket match in progress.

St. Andrews is a remarkable golf course and a very good one. It lies in a narrow valley between thick-wooded hills reminiscent of Malaya and Penang, and, as you turn in to the club-house, you find yourself remarking that surely there cannot be eighteen holes. In fact there are, and a most enjoyable and authentic game of golf they afford, with a par of 68 and a length of less than 6,000 yards. It makes you wonder what on earth we are doing at home playing with a ball that causes us to walk upwards of 7,000 yards and be hard put to it to get in two rounds in a day.

I have always suspected that the late Harry Colt was the best golf architect of all time. He designed Pine Valley and many of our own finest courses, which I will not enumerate at this distance, in case I get one wrong, but I doubt whether he ever did anything better than St. Andrews, Trinidad—if only because he never in fact set eyes on it. They sent him some contour maps and some aerial photographs and he sat down and laid it out at a range of 4,000 miles. Apart from recently altering the tee of one short hole—which, contrary to what usually happens when club committees usurp the functions of the golf architect, is a great improvement—it remains exactly as he designed it from afar in 1934.

It possesses, however, one really splendid hazard which I am sure that neither Colt, nor for that matter any other golf architect, ever visualized. On an embankment adjacent to several of the greens and tees they have a rifle range.

The silence as a man concentrates on the crucial tee-shot or five-foot putt may at any moment be broken by a shattering report which echoes and reverberates among the hills in a manner calculated to recall to any 14th Army veteran his finest hour. As you stand there, brooding over your stroke, it is bad enough when it does go off, and you have an excuse. It is infinitely worse when it doesn't and you haven't.

It was borne in upon me on my first visit to Persia in 1944 that those who go out into the wilds in search of oil habitually do three things; erect a tent, set up their drilling gear, and lay out nine holes—in that order. Since Palo Seco in Southern Trinidad, where British Petroleum now have an interest, can by no stretch of imagination be called the wilds, they have been understandably lax in this matter, but are now repairing the omission. The scene is to be 50 acres of low bush interspersed with what the architects call 'features'—a winding stream, undulations in the ground, a variety of wonderful tall trees, a number of tethered cows, and a squatter growing bananas.

From this could be made without doubt the finest nine-hole course in the Tropics, and great was the temptation when hints were thrown out that I might care to stay and take a hand in it. Only an idiot or an outstanding conscientious and hardworking writer leaves the West Indies for an English November. Thus it comes about that the latter is now seated in the commodious tail of the B.O.A.C. Stratocruiser *Cleopatra* being borne only too rapidly towards the rubbish dumps and flooded gravel pits of Staines, which welcome the returning Englishman to his happy homeland.

The connection to Montego Bay was an hour late and there were moments when the prospect of a couple of days' delay in the Noel Coward country passed hopefully through the mind, but, alas, the faithful *Cleopatra* had awaited our coming. So now there is nothing for it. Back to work. If past experience be any guide, the sneezing will start tomorrow, the shivering on Tuesday, and by Wednesday we shall be safely between the sheets with the doctor in daily attendance.

Liberty, Sorority, Equality!

It appears that in my recent absence abroad a number of letters reached this office from frustrated ladies deploring their continued lowly status in the local golf club. Members of Parliament are only too familiar with the barrage of postal protests which arrive simultaneously from all parts of the country, every letter by a singular coincidence couched in identical terms, and I am sure that all Hon. and Rt. Hon. Gentlemen, as they cast them into the waste-paper basket, spare a sympathetic thought for the diligence with which the writers sat down and copied out the circular.

In the present case the variety of expression suggests no such collusion and the Ladies' Golf Unions are hereby acquitted of being the spider in a sinister web of propaganda. It seems that a great many women golfers do indeed feel sore at not being allowed to play on Sundays and at being kept in a separate tent, as it were, like the female Bedouin Arab. The spirit of revolt seethes throughout the land. At any moment we shall find a couple of golfing Pankhursts chained to the railings of the Royal and Ancient, and I only hope I am there to see it.

The truth is that women golfers have never, in this country at least, been taken with a seriousness which they do not deserve. In America the sight of Miss Patty Berg running a couple of miles every morning in a track suit to strengthen her legs for golf excites nothing but admiration—though tinged in my own case by the thought that it brought her last year in prize money alone rather more than the salary of a British Cabinet Minister. Here at home such a spectacle would excite that uneasy mixture of respect and regret which so many of us experience at the circus.

The cross which women golfers in this country have to bear is not so much that they cannot play on Sundays—though I dare say a good many clubs would let them if they paid the same subscription as the men—but that, like mothers-in-law, they are the butt of innumerable jokes, most of them as feeble as the one about practising for the mixed foursomes. Furthermore, it is assumed by those who know no better that they (a) habitually cheat, and (b) are possessed of what a colleague of mine once described as 'billiard table legs, leathery faces, and clumsy great paws'. You have only to look at the golfing girls of today to see that at least the latter charge is grossly unfair.

Having most of my life been a rabid segregationist, I have now mellowed—or ratted, whichever way you like to look at it—into an equally rabid integrationist. I like to see the sexes intermingle in the club-house. I think the time has passed when the ladies on a Sunday morning should go in by a separate entrance and be confined to a small back room, there to engage in outward pleasantries and dark inward thoughts, tapping their tiny feet while they pluck up courage to send a message through to the lord and master—whose own finest hour with his witty friends is being spoiled, if they only knew it, by the call of conscience and covert glances to see if the steward is approaching with the dread summons.

It may perhaps be no coincidence that three of the happiest clubs I know have only one main room and the question of apartheid therefore does not arise, but this, of course, is every club's domestic affair and only becomes anyone else's business when a championship or some such is played on its course. In this case I do solemnly declare that any club unwilling to open wide its portals on that occasion should, with suitable thanks and regret, decline the championship.

To come 6,000 miles to play in a British championship, as some of our Dominions and American friends do, and find that your wife cannot meet you in the club-house is surely no longer to be endured.

All moralists, however, feel entitled to make what I believe Charles I called 'mental reservations' in their own favour and in this instance I unhesitatingly make one in mine, namely the holy of holies at St. Andrews, where, in any case, there are a women's club and plenty of hotels adjacent to the eighteenth green. As it would be improper for me to comment upon the internal affairs of the R. and A., I content myself with quoting the words of a senior member twenty-odd years ago on observing for the first time a woman cashier in the dining-room.

'Damn it,' he said, 'it's a woman. Last woman I saw in here was an American. She was smoking. In the silence room. I soon had 'er out.'

Long may such stalwarts live to defend this particular citadel. As to the others, let the gates be thrown open and the barricades unmanned. Liberty, sorority, equality!

Black Feat

Every day our pride seems destined to be deflated in ways both great and small. Our gallant allies on their usual grand scale stage a misfirework display that can only bring to mind the instructions engraved on every schoolboy's memory, 'Light the blue touchpaper and retire immediately', while the Russians on the other side of the fence bring near to reality the tale that has been going the rounds for some time now, concerning the two Russian scientists at the pearly gates, who, on being declined admission, replied, 'We don't want to come in. We only want our ball back'.

Now, more properly within the province of this column, I have to report that, following on the victory of the Japanese over the rest of the world at golf in 1957, a Kikuyu caddie has won a competition at the Royal Nairobi Club with 18 consecutive pars and a total of 73. My informant passes on the news from a friend in Kenya who marked his card. 'I have never seen anything like it,' he writes—and I apologize on his behalf for some faintly derogatory observations upon a number of eminent professionals—'he had imitated the style of Bobby Barr, our pro., to perfection, but his short game was much superior. Into the bargain, he played like all the others with four clubs only: a number two wood, Nos. four and eight irons and a putter.

'To see him use his four when he really wanted a six reminded me of the art of the old golfing generation developed when I was a youngster instead of having a battery of fourteen clubs. His short game was quite immaculate and he took 25 putts for the round. And to cap it all he made an excellent speech, which could not have been bettered by anyone.'

The winner, being ignorant, reasonably enough, of the somewhat complicated definitions of amateur status and in particular the clause about carrying clubs for hire after the age of sixteen, expressed the hope that soon he and his fellow caddie-enthusiasts would be playing in the Amateur. My friend seeks to get round this by forming a Kikuyu artisan section—splendid thought!—which would be affiliated to the Golfing Union of Kenya. 'We have progressed a long way,' he concludes, 'from the time twenty years ago when Arthur H—— and I played two caddies, got beaten, and very nearly had to resign from the club.'

Perhaps I am getting crusty, but anything which reduces the artificial complications of the golf swing and in particular the solemnity with which the game so often seems to be taken always appeals to me. I take this big black fellow's feat in doing every hole in par with four clubs, and that of the three caddies in Colombo who, I remember, when I was there, had just done level fours with bare feet and three clubs apiece, as a corrective not merely to the members of their distinguished patron clubs but to all of us.

For instance I yield to no one in my admiration for Sam Snead's golf swing. I have a coloured movie, which I have seen dozens of times and still enjoy, which I took at the Thunderbird Club in California during the 1955 Ryder Cup match in America. A line of professionals are practising side by side, their clubs glinting as they flash swiftly in the brilliant desert sunshine. In the centre, one of them seems almost to be playing in slow motion and this, of course, is Snead. Nevertheless, though this is indeed the poetry of motion, what I should most dearly love to have seen in all Snead's career was the round he played with a tree trunk.

This occurred some years ago at his home club, White Sulphur Springs, Virginia, when he disappeared into the woods and came out with a small tree which he carved by hand into the form of a golf club—thus proving himself, incidentally, one of the last club-maker-professionals left in America.

With this, plus, it is true, a wedge, he holed the course in 76.

Such deplorable frivolity will shock the solemnly dedicated golfer—the kind at which those masters of deflation, Stephen Leacock and P. G. Wodehouse, have poked such splendid fun. With what delight, I thought, would they have been present in a railway carriage the other day in Japan, when four of us were on our way from Tokyo to sample the local edition of Gleneagles at Kawana. The train was making its way along a coast line that put the South of France in the shade, winding its way round little bays fringed with fir trees and burrowing through tunnels to emerge upon a scene even more enchanting on the other side. Inland, terrace after terrace of tangerine groves graced the hillsides. Marvelling at the idyllic beauty of the scene, we passed some trees in blossom with flowers of a particularly delicate shade of pinkish orange. They were, our Japanese companion said, persimmon.

'Ah,' said the Dedicated Golfer, 'that's what they use for making wooden clubs.'

'Christmas Trees'

Nothing could be more seasonably appropriate than a letter I have received from the founder of the milk supply of the city of Khartoum. Now presumably in retirement, he writes from Brockenhurst, and his theme is trees. Such a subject would hardly have arisen on the last occasion on which we met at the Khartoum Golf Club, when, in partnership with the head of the Technical College, I remember beating my friend and the Director of Mechanical Transport. It is my recollection that on this sandy waste, hard beside the Blue Nile and within a mile or two of where Sir Winston made his celebrated cavalry charge at Omdurman, there grow no trees at all—unless you glorify by that name the revolting camel thorn, whose spikes, though much relished by that animal, go straight through your shoe and are commonly used as gramophone needles.

Brockenhurst Manor, on the other hand, is full of trees, as befits a golf course in the New Forest, but its committee feel that it might with advantage be fuller and have hit upon the ingenious thought that individual members might care to donate a tree to perpetuate their memory when they are gone. Each tree will be labelled with three items of information—the name of the donor, the name of the tree, and the date (whether of the planting of the tree or the decease of the donor is not stated).

No member is to give more than one tree and no species is to be duplicated, so it is to be a case of first come first served —not, be it noted, 'first gone'. One gallant colonel is reported to have 'brightened visibly', since he now knows what to do, or have done, with his ashes; they will be scattered under the silver spruce which he has earmarked for planting between the ninth and the sixteenth.

A lady member, harking back subconsciously perhaps to her most distant ancestor, has chosen an apple tree. She likes to think that, long after she has departed, juvenile and delinquent descendants of Adam will enjoy stealing the fruit.

This charming scheme, worthy of emulation by so many golf clubs whom it would be uncharitable to mention so near to Christmas, set me at once in mind of that great tree lover, Dr. John R. Williams, President of the Oak Hill Club at Rochester, N.Y. In 1949 the club dedicated a fine Pin Oak, or *Quercus Palustris*, to commemorate the visit of the British Walker Cup team, and later in the year Dr. Williams sent a number of its acorns—via the diplomatic bag from Washington ('acorns will not germinate if allowed to dry')—to the British captain, P. B. Lucas. These were duly distributed to the home clubs of the members of the team.

'In six to eight years,' said the doctor, 'you will have some fine beautiful trees which may be set out in permanent location.' Eight years have now gone by and I am happy to report that some at least have fulfilled the pious donor's hopes. Research at the time told me that the Pin Oak has never been found in Scotland or Ireland, so it is not surprising that from little acorns nothing grew in those two countries, though I believe the Scottish ones showed their heads and immediately withdrew.

Of *Querci* Ronnie White, Ernest Millward, and Arthur Perowne at Hoylake, Bournemouth and Norwich respectively I have no information, but I can certify that the captain's are doing well at Sandy Lodge, one in the rough on the left of the first and the other on the right of the twelfth, and hopes are even entertained of that enthusiastic golfer, Mr. John Whitney, the American Ambassador, to affix a ceremonial plaque upon them now that they are three feet high.

Several *Querci* Gerald Micklem have grown to adolescence at Wildernese and survived transplanting when the new club-house was built, while the Max McCready specimen at Sunningdale, after two years in the little garden on the right of the practice green, grew out of the nursery stage and is now beside the 14th tee, where it has grown to five feet.

All this, if not strictly related to Christmas, strikes me as a conception well in keeping with the spirit of the moment, and, if golf club secretaries are bombarded with catalogues by enterprising nurserymen, I do not care. I have only one improvement to suggest. At Brockenhurst they are to be allowed to choose what they plant. I think we should be allowed to choose where we plant. I can think of a dozen spots where I might plant mine, happy in the knowledge that, for maybe a hundred years after I am gone, infuriated golfers would be bent double taking trial backswings under its branches and reading: 'H. Longhurst. *Crataegus Punctata*. 25 December 1957'.

Bending the Elbow

The 1957 captain of the Royal and Ancient Golf Club does it. The chairman of the Championship Committee does it. The chairman of the Rules of Golf Committee does it. Even the woman champion of England does it. We may therefore deduce that there must surely be something to it. And what is this common practice that binds together so distinguished a quartet—to say nothing of an increasing number of commoner fry? Why, the fact that they all putt like croquet players instead of golfers, and are in imminent danger of being allowed to do so no more.

There are, of course, variants of croquet-golfers just as there are variants among croquet players proper. What we may perhaps call the 'normal'—if only because, as I take it they were the first—are the between-the-legs exponents, who clasp their mallet-headed club at the top of the shaft with one hand and hold it about half-way down with the other.

This is the method long favoured by the captain of the R. and A., who the other day, I cannot forbear to add, putted into his hat—though this was nothing to do with the method. In a challenge match at Sandwich, with 'this for a half' at the seventeeth, John Beck's hat was blown off in the course of the stroke and the ball actually went into it, thus making him the first known golfer who in truth could hit his hat.

Others, among whom Leonard Crawley is perhaps the pioneer, favour the more decorous vicarage-tea-party stroke, with the right foot withdrawn and the ball propelled from beside the left.

Thirdly, and so far as I know completely new, is what may be called the long-arm method. Which arm does not matter, though normally it is the right, but the point is that it is fully extended. The club is held high up with one hand and the player, leaning down, clutches it within an inch or two of the bottom with the other, giving the ball a decisive hammer-like prod with his straight lower arm.

There comes a point when all of us must risk writs for libel in the cause of Truth, so I must now reveal that many croquet-putters—no, hang it, most croquet-putters (in for a penny, in for a thousand pounds!)—take to this method because they have contracted that dire golfing disease known as the 'jitters' to such a degree that they can no longer face short putts in the ordinary way. Should this be their dilemma, let them (a) take to the long-arm method and (b) derive consolation from the thought that they are not alone in their misery.

Some time ago when I wrote about the 'jitters'—and there are those so susceptible that they cannot bear to read of it, as others cannot bear to see the word 'socketing' in print—a doctor told me that he had specialized in the subject. It was all a mattter of the nerves in the angle of the elbow, he said.

Most of us will have seen the man who has difficulty in raising a glass to his lips. With the arm fully extended he can hold it steady, or with the arm clutched closely to the shoulder, supported in extreme cases by a handkerchief acting as a sling. It is the bent elbow period between that upsets both the man and the contents of his glass—and the latter may well, for that matter, be water.

Similarly, I shall not readily forget the experience of my partner—a particularly sober fellow—before the University match foursomes many years ago. Nerves were on edge, it was a bitter morning, and he had unwittingly ordered grapefruit for his breakfast. Section by section was safely lodged in the spoon, but none reached its destination. As the elbow bent, some were jerked limply on to the table-cloth, others shot over the left shoulder as though in dropping a provisional ball.

Worst of all, according to my doctor friend, is the thought that violinists get it! They can do the twiddly bits—I fear I am no musician—with the arm fully extended, and the other bits just under the chin, but when it comes to the bits in the middle, a convulsive twitch nearly saws the appliance in half.

Having myself suffered hideously from a malady which may sound ludicrous to others but which has driven many a better man to give up golf altogether, I almost wish I had never mentioned the subject. More especially as some of those who have derived a new golfing life from playing croquet-fashion are the very people who are now, in consultation with the United States, faced with deciding whether it should be banned forthwith from the game.

T-Square

Opinion upon the ethics of the golfers who putt as though they were playing croquet, of whom I was recently writing, seems strong, but divided. On the one side, 'We don't do anybody any harm. Why should not we be allowed to continue our innocent pleasure?' On the other, 'Gad, sir. If this is golf, sir . . . and what are the Royal and Ancient going to do about it?'

If I revert to the subject, it is to say to both of them, 'Wait a moment. You ain't seen nothing yet.' I refer to the invention of that self-styled crank, and potential benefactor of the human race, Mr. Percy J. Gillespie, of Dublin.

His invention is a putter to end all putters—and I have a sneaking suspicion that, unless it were banned, it might. I think it is common ground that the ideal putting stroke, if ever it could be achieved, would be that of a pendulum. For this we can quote two distinguished authorities, one theoretical, the other practical. The first is none other than Bobby Jones.

'Unquestionably,' he wrote, 'a pendulum-like swing, precisely along the line of the putt and suspended from a point exactly over the ball, furnishes the ideal conception of accurate striking. But so long as human toes stick out in front and until a golf club turns into a croquet mallet and can be swung backward between the legs, there is little hope of this being attained.'

The practical man was Lord Brabazon of Tara, who once constructed an automatic putter. This was a heavy tripod, with swinging pendulum and various gadgets to ensure one putt being struck with precisely the same strength and direction as another. He tried first at six feet. 'It may startle you to know,' he reported, 'that at six feet you can stay there all day and every single one will go in, without exception, for the whole afternoon. Never mind what the slope of the green is. Once you have set your machine right the ball will go in. Every time.'

He then tried from 12 feet, and from here, over a long period, 20 out of every 21 went in. Incidentally, the American ball did better, with 24 out of 25. We may therefore assume that the pendulum theory is correct.

Unfortunately, however, no one hitherto has discovered any true pendulum possible within the limits of the human frame, for a pendulum will only swing truly either from a fixed point, as in a clock, or when slung from a couple of 'arms' of exactly equal length. This rules out all forms of putting where, by virtue of the grip, one human arm is longer than the other, by however little.

Mr. Gillespie has discovered the one position in which both human arms are the same length—namely, leaning down, clasping a very short club with the two thumbs exactly level, and propelling the ball forward, stiff-elbowed and stiff-wristed, from between the legs. His putter—if such it may be called—is like an elongated T-square, with an ordinary flat handle two feet long and $1\frac{1}{4}$ inches wide and the top of the 'T' about four inches across. The thumbs lie side by side on the handle, facing forwards, and the fingers intertwine, as though in an attitude of prayer, at the back.

Some months ago he sent me one. After absorbing the theory from the accompanying handbook and practising on the carpet, I took it down to the local club, where the 18th green is in a sort of hollow, and after looking furtively around to see that no one was about I leant down and had a go. I had four balls and set them down between four and five feet from the hole.

The first four went in, clean as a whistle. So did the next. Even when I pretended that the last one was 'This for the Open Championship', the third four went in and so did the fourth. The 19th missed—mainly because I was getting frightened at the enormity of what I was doing—but I holed the 20th. Nineteen out of 20!

Later, at varying lengths, I would be getting along splendidly when one would shoot suddenly out to the right of the hole—not sliced but straight there. When I realized what was wrong, it served only to confirm the theory. Instinct, I found, had caused the right thumb to creep slightly down the shaft, perhaps half an inch lower than the left. So the two arms of the pendulum were no longer the same length and the apparatus was out of true.

The whole thing to me has been a remarkable revelation. Joe Carr, I am told, became a past master at it but had not the nerve to do it in public, while Harry Bradshaw has told me the inventor himself is 'dead from 10 feet'—very much after the fashion, as Bofors gunners of the last war may recall, of Colonel Kerrison and his No. 3 Predictor.

All good things come to an end, they say, and here I have fears for Mr. Gillespie and his T-square, a specimen of which is now in the hands of the Rules of Golf Committee. It conforms without doubt to the more precise definitions of a golf club, but whether it will survive the ominous words 'a club shall not be substantially different from the traditional and customary form and make' remains to be seen. If not, it deserves at least a place of honour in the R. and A. museum —'the only one that really worked'.[1]

---

[1] Lloyds, on being assured that the putter would not be banned, insured Mr. Gillespie for £1,000 against this happening. Within a matter of weeks it was in fact banned and he 'collected'.

Guilty Conscience

As I bask in the mellow sunshine on the terrace, I reflect that there is no smugness to equal that of the Englishman who for some respectable purpose has retreated from his native land just at the precise meteorological moment.

The overseas news service of the B.B.C., which, incidentally, is most human and entertaining by comparison with the domestic edition, tells us of Arctic conditions at home and the local paper reports 18 inches of snow falling in southern England in one night. A misprint, maybe, but there must have been a tidy amount—enough certainly to ensure that those of my household left at home are already semaphoring to the Cuckfield Rural District Council for the snow plough to come and get them out.

The terrace on which these unworthy thoughts come to my mind is that of the Royal Baghdad Golf Club, where I confess to having been received with a positively embarrassing warmth of welcome. The course, as all are at pains to point out, is not in its finest condition. Being completely flat, it has harboured the overnight rain and this has turned the alluvial deposit of which it, and indeed most of Iraq, is formed into— well, frankly, mud.

Still, we have had a most enjoyable, if to me, somewhat humbling game. This is a form of golf which demands great accuracy of striking, to say nothing of a certain low cunning in the short game unattainable by the newcomer and, being somewhat out of practice, my false reputation has been properly exposed. The ball must be taken absolutely clean. To touch the earth first, be it ever so slightly, results in the club being snatched from one's grasp, leaving a few fingers of each hand attached lightly to the grip, as though in playing the flute. The ball, together with a shower of alluvial deposit, goes about 20 yards.

There is, however, a singular compensation in playing at Baghdad, for it is completely enclosed by the racecourse. It is as though one transferred the Newmarket Links across the Cambridge Road and set it down against the rails opposite the grandstand. At any rate, in the course of our game we were able to watch three races from start to finish and indeed to enjoy a little moment of triumph.

It is the habit of the jockeys to ride half-way to the start and then to dismount and walk, enjoying a smoke and a chat on the way—this being to allow the citizens time to place their bets on the totalizator, which they wisely decline to do until they have confirmed with their own eyes that their selection is present on the course, in possession of four legs and duly mounted by a jockey. Thus it was that, as we tee-ed up for the short seventh, no fewer than four jockeys had stopped to see the fun and were leaning over the rails a few yards away.

All of them, like jockeys in every part of the world, bore a striking resemblance to my old friend, Charlie Smirke—except that they wear coloured scarves in the back of their caps, which flow out in the wind during the race in fine Lawrence of Arabia fashion—and all of them, so help me, were clearly smirking.

One might not understand their comments, but could hardly fail to get the gist of them. Whereupon three of us put our tee shots right in the middle of the green and my partner, Alan Bell, who I believe once played in the boys' international for Scotland, hit the stick with a resounding crack and nearly holed in one. We sauntered from the tee without turning round, rather with the air of the gentleman in the top hat who has been missed by a small boy with a snowball.

Later, after watching another race from the golf club terrace, where the horses charge past within the length of a longish putt from one's table, we walked down the racecourse to the centre of operations to take a tilt at the totalizator. My host, Brig. P. G. Wreford Brown, being a steward of the meeting, to say nothing of being also the Military Attaché, I could hardly seek enlightenment from that quarter, but I did succeed in having my card marked by what I was assured to be the most inspired source in Baghdad.

Not a single selection finished in the first ten, but that only goes to show that inspired sources do not vary much from one part of the world to the other.

What remains in my mind is a mixed feeling of guilt—partly to be sitting here in the sunshine at all and partly because I once wrote, after visiting Baghdad for the first time during the war, 'If this is the city of a thousand and one nights, then, having had the one, I will let anyone else have the other thousand'. Now, having had five, I leave with the utmost regret in the morning.

One Foot Wrong

In a moderately wide experience of games I have come to conclude that none produces such moments of personal mortification as golf. Being bowled by a full toss, missing a sitting goal, and such like, are bad enough in their way but at least somebody else was engaged in the operation. In golf you have it all to yourself. Such thoughts occurred to me as I stood recently in a small sand bunker in Kuwait.

It was not so much the fact that on a course surrounded by a thousand miles of sand in almost every direction I had driven into the one small patch in which I was unable to ground my club; it was the knowledge—still in the forefront of my mind, since I had been informed only on the previous hole—that it had been put there by my old Halford Hewitt partner, Mr. J. S. F. Morrison. The mocking comments he would have been making, and will doubtless make when next we meet, were ringing in my ears as I played.

Nevertheless, from material not wholly designed by Providence for a golf course, I confess that he did an excellent job, and, with a stiff breeze blowing in from the Persian Gulf, many of the holes, and especially the tee shots, bear a most authentic air.

If he should tire of the golf, the newcomer, not yet so familiar with the scene as to take it for granted, may always gaze down with awe at one of the wonders of the world, namely, its biggest filling station. The tankers come in eight at a time and with a simplicity which makes the operation intelligible even to me are filled up and sent on their way, for all the world like motor-cars at a wayside garage at home.

The only difference is that the answer to 'How many, sir?' is liable to be not four gallons but 80,000 tons. The similarity is increased, however, by the fact that tanker skippers—like the owners of so many modern British cars whose designers seem to have overlooked the fact that when petrol goes into the tank air must come out—nearly always add, 'And don't put it in too fast'.

My wanderings amid blue waters, sand and sunshine being connected with recording something in celebration of the first fifty years of British Petroleum, have naturally brought me into contact mainly with what are often known, as though they were somehow a race apart, which indeed they are not, as 'oilmen'. They have also brought home the truth of a remark made light-heartedly to me some years ago, which I may have quoted before, namely, that those who go out in search of oil habitually do three things—set up something to live in, erect their drilling gear, and lay out nine holes in that order.

No better example could be found than a hitherto un-heard-of patch of rock and sand called Das Island, which juts imperceptibly out of the middle of the Gulf, little more than a mile long and three-quarters of a mile wide. Uninhabited throughout recorded history, it is now the base for a fantastic drilling barge, which was towed out here some 7,000 miles and stands in the sea on four gigantic legs twenty miles from the island.

On Das, as well as among the fifty men living on the barge, the accents of Scotland predominate, but even I was sur-prised on stepping out of the aeroplane to be greeted with the inevitable 'You must come and inspect our golf course'. I was also a little taken aback at being greeted by Mr. Terry-Thomas, the film-actor—with whom on the mainland at Bahrein I assisted, sitting cross-legged, in eating a sheep.

It seemed impossible that after accommodating 400

people, to say nothing of all their equipment and an airstrip, this barren outpost of Scotland could make room also for a golf course but already, after only three months, there it was with the nine tees all built, the fairways ready for the bulldozer, the greens marked out, and three Indian tailors hard at work embroidering nine flags with the company's emblem.

Furthermore, with only a slight change of plan, they have a chance, hard beside the waves breaking over the rocky northern shore, of making a hole as majestic and photogenic as the celebrated sixteenth at Cypress Point in California.

As my journey draws, alas, towards its close, I look back with wonder at the absolute determination of people to play this strange game wherever life may cast them. Their company and their hospitality have been a great delight and I like to feel that I have only put one foot wrong. This was in one of the oilfields of Persia, where the bulldozers were hard at work on some fine rolling territory of which any golf architect would approve.

In charge—shades of the old days!—was a Mr. Graef, from San Antonio, Texas, the club president. 'What do you think of flat fairways?' he said. '—— awful!' I naturally replied. This was the wrong thing. Mr. Graef, it transpired, being a good construction engineer with vast implements of destruction at his command, was having to be almost forcibly restrained from flattening the entire course out like an airfield.

First Principles

I often think that one's attitude to the game of golf is subconsciously conditioned for a lifetime by the circumstances in which one is first introduced to it. Those of us who see it first in its most elementary, primitive form, knocking a ball along with one club, or perhaps even two or three, cheerfully encountering all manner of unorthodox hazards on the way until eventually we get it into the hole, seem to me to have captured a basic outlook on the game which can never later be revealed to those who travelled first class from the start.

My own beginnings were primitive in the extreme. I was introduced to the game before breakfast one morning on the common at Yelverton, Devon, by two other small boys whose parents were taking their holiday in the same hotel. They had devised a triangular course of three holes—no tees, flags, fairways or any other such nonsense, of course—and with luck we could get in two rounds before breakfast.

None of us, therefore, were baptized in the faith that, if we drove on to the fairway, we were entitled to a 'fairway lie', and that, if we did not get it, we had been robbed. Ours was a simple creed. You played the ball where you found it. The only true disaster in golf was when you could not find it.

During the last month, and especially during the long

twenty-six hours which it took us to fly home from Aden, these thoughts have been much in my mind. In that period I played on or visited eight courses, and on only one of them is a shot ever likely to be played off grass.

Yet in many a case the challenge to the player seemed more authentic, more like the original game of golf, than what we have come to expect on the super-sophisticated courses at home.

On desert courses the shot is always 'on'. There is always some way of stopping on the green, or turning three shots into two from just off it, but the way is not revealed, as it is at home, by merely asking, 'What club is it?' Much crafty thought must be devoted to the problem, and every shot, as Henry Cotton has so well put it, must be 'manufactured'. Indeed, it has often struck me that he would be a past master at this form of golf, whereas the machine-like Hogan might well be a total loss.

The reforming spirits who crusade for Simpler Golf would find their case strengthened in these remote parts. Though the veneer of sophistication has crept outwards, to such an extent that some enthusiasts carry a full set of fourteen gleaming and expensive clubs, the truth is soon brought home that all you need, between the driver and the putter, is three—a mover-onner, a pusher-upper and a getter-outer. For good value you could perhaps add that favourite club of our grandfathers, the rut-iron.

At Aden, where all is sand, alternately firm and powdery—except the asphalt greens, which are rolled by a supercilious camel—they entertained me most kindly and in the course of presenting me with a tankard to commemorate the visit observed deferentially that it 'wasn't quite like the Old course at St. Andrews'. Yet only a moment before I had been remarking to the captain of the club that it was.

This is not to be taken as suggesting that the Old course resembles a patch of sand—though heaven knows some pretty hard things have been said about it in recent years—but merely to indicate that the two places had in common not only the accents of Fife but the supreme quality of forcing the golfer to stop before every shot and think out precisely what he was trying to do and how he was going to do it.

In both cases the reward of success is correspondingly greater. To manœuvre the ball on to the eleventh green at St. Andrews, with a strong following wind and the flag tucked away behind the bunker, is not merely to 'get on the green at the short eleventh,' as it would be on most courses. It makes you wish that Vardon had been there to see you do it.

To cause a ball to carry an expanse of loose sand and pitch on a firm patch with just the right trajectory to run up through the gully and come to rest on a small circle of fast-running asphalt is a stroke every bit as worthy of the master's approval.

You cannot blame the youthful would-be champions of today if they imagine that golf at its best involves flawless fairways, billiard table greens, carefully raked bunkers—in case anyone were inconvenienced by having got into them—£70 worth of bag and clubs and a four-course lunch. A spell in the desert would reveal that these are but the fleshpots of golf.

The Day

In the good old days when the gentry were the gentry and an amateur never practised, the upper crust of golfers, so far as I can gather, simply did not reckon to play in winter. Some put their clubs away on the opening day of the partridge season, while others lingered on to enjoy September at North Berwick, where they would be photographed by Mr. Balmain for the shiny shilling weeklies as they sat beside the wall, waiting in the hold-up on the 16th tee.

These connoisseurs had created a welfare state of their own, on which, far from being jealous, I allow my mind to dwell with nostalgic contentment. They shot pheasant and hunted foxes till Christmas and then pushed off into the sunshine. Nevertheless, as the winter turned at last, there will have come to those who were true golfers at heart an experience which we lesser mortals year by year can share.

That is what I have long since known in my own mind as '*The* Day'. Like Easter, it has no fixed place in the calender. Sometimes it is early, always with the possibility of its being a false alarm, and sometimes it is an unconscionable time a-coming; but come eventually it does.

'*The* Day' has certain indispensable qualities. The sun must be shining, the primroses must be out, it must be warm enough to play in a sleeveless pullover and the greens must have been mown—partly because of the first scent of new-mown grass and partly to see the sun glistening on the criss-cross pattern left by the mower.

It is a moment when faith returns after an English winter, the world is good, and one might even take a few swings with the patent heavy-headed short club that has so long been lying idle in the umbrella stand—thus discovering that, far from having a firm grip with the last two fingers of the left hand, as laid down in the text books, one has none at all.

The conception crystallized in the minds of two of us simultaneously many years ago, and I recall the scene as though it were yesterday. We were basking in the sun outside the White Horse on the Great North Road near Eaton Socon, attired in the 'co-respondent' shoes that were then the order of the day, and soon were due to play together in the University match at Rye. My companion furthermore was due, though he can hardly have suspected it at the time, to be Amateur Champion within two years—Eric Martin Smith.

Since then I have lived to enjoy '*The* Day' in a rich variety of places, and can remember nearly all of them. Two came at Sandwich, with the larks singing and the white cliffs shining across the bay—a scene on which one has waxed lyrical perhaps too often. Another was on the Downs at Royal Eastbourne—a form of architecturally 'bad' golf, as downland golf is always declared to be, to which I am particularly addicted—more especially when I look down from the first fairway and savour the fact that I am now one of those golfers silhouetted on the skyline, at whom, as a small boy at school, one used to look up with furtive envy.

Perhaps the most memorable day occurred at Saunton, where the tulip farms were already ablaze and other parts of England were reported to be under snow. Yet another recalls a neighbouring scene across the bay at Westward Ho! with the Burrows, as they call the flat expanse on which that great course lies, gleaming placidly in the spring sunshine.

Looking down from his bungalow on that same scene this morning will be J. H. Taylor, and this reminds me that this is

OOS–I

a great week for birthdays—what with St. Patrick's tomorrow, mine on Tuesday (one more for the half-century), and J. H.'s on Wednesday, when he will be eighty-seven, just sixty-four years since he won the first of his five open championships.

What a wonderful life he has had, and is still enjoying—writing in his determined and still flawless hand to enter the controversies of the day, defending what was good in the old and welcoming what is good in the new.

When he started as the smallest of the caddie boys at Westward Ho! rushing to offer his services to such august figures as Horace Hutchinson and the school-masters whose memory was perpetuated by Kipling in *Stalky and Co.*, the fee was sixpence a round, minus threepence if you lost a ball. Now he is president of the club.

I hope indeed that '*The* Day' will come this week and for 'J. H.'s' sake, as golfers all over the world send him their good wishes, let it be Wednesday.

Nonconformist

I find myself hailing Harry Bradshaw's victory in the
P. G. A. close championship[1] with much pleasure and a wry
smile. When Commonwealth pirates like Locke, Thomson,
Von Nida, Player and Wilkes so persistently snatched the
bread from the mouths of honest men who could not play
golf quite so well, the P. G. A. invented this tournament to
ensure that the winner of at least one event should be a
home product.

It seems however, that, in order to realize this laudable
ambition, they will have to make their close championship
closer still, for two out of the first four, including the winner,
turned out to be raiders from the Republic of Eire!

Be that as it may, to watch Bradshaw winning anything,
any time, anywhere is a satisfying experience. We are always
being told that we live today in a 'conforming' society—an
odious conception if ever there was one!—and it has long
struck me that this is becoming more and more true of what
should surely have remained the most individualistic of all
games, namely golf. Whatever else our Harry may do, he
certainly does not conform. He is, in fact, the complete
nonconformist.

His grip almost defies analysis and is certainly unique in

[1] 1958.

that the first two fingers of his right hand hang down like bananas and appear to play no part in the stroke at all. As for keeping the head still, I estimate, from deliberate observation of this point, that his head moves between 12 and 15 inches in the course of the stroke and that, at the moment of striking, the ball must appear to be moving rapidly backwards. His swing I once described as 'agricultural' and, despite outraged protests from across the water on that occasion, I can find no better word.

Harry Bradshaw's method has, however, one indisputable merit. It works. I shall not readily forget the polite astonishment with which it was first viewed during the 1955 Ryder Cup match played at Thunderbird, in the Californian desert. Nothing like this, either in technique or in his general approach to the game, had been seen in those parts before—unless perhaps in the person of Mr. John Montague, the man said to play to par with a baseball bat, rake and shovel, whom incidentally I met at Thunderbird.

Ambling genially round, ever ready to exchange a cheerful word with those who had come to watch, and hitting each shot before the average American professional would have had time to test the direction of a non-existent wind, Bradshaw holed the course in 65, the lowest single round on either side.

The thought comes to me—and I trust that no religious significance will attach to it—that perhaps Eire is the last citadel of the nonconformists. Joe Carr, for instance, takes a fine individualistic slash at the ball, and when he reaches the green either straddles down, like a giraffe settling down to drink, and uses a putter which rises little higher than his knee, or, having discarded it once again in disgust, putts with a 3-iron.

James Bruen, who I dare say hit the ball as far as any man alive in his day, 'looped' the club so that at one point in the backswing it was pointing directly over the tee box, and furthermore, was twice known to break a club under the handle in the course of the down swing before ever it had reached the ground.

Uniformity is now the order of the day and, while no two men play precisely alike, I think it is fair to say that there is today, perhaps for the first time in history, a recognized 'correct' method at which all are aiming. I am sure this is very worthy, and all that, but it is still the individualist who provides the colour and the fun.

What fun it was, for instance, to see Ted Ray, with his felt hat turned up at the front and his pipe aglow, bashing at the ball as hard as mortal man could hit it and gouging the turf from the tee where his heels had twisted. Or to watch Leo Diegel, who put the verb 'to Diegel' into the golfing language of the 'thirties, putting with outstretched elbows and the top of the club pressing against the third button of his waistcoat.

Abe Mitchell, quiet and reserved as he was, had a style all his own, whereby he anchored his right foot square to the hole and gave the ball a tremendous blow with his hand and arms. His was perhaps the simplest style of all the great players, with the possible exception of Gene Sarazen's—so simple in fact that it ruined half a Cambridge team of my time, till one day a couple of us set our wrists beside his for comparison. They looked like matchsticks.

In the present climate there could hardly flourish another Walter Hagen, perhaps the supreme nonconformist of all time. He is too often described as a 'showman', which indeed he was—in the days when a showman reckoned to put on a show, not merely get himself involved in a row[1]—but the truth is that his golfing style was also highly individualistic. 'They always said I started my shots with a sway and ended with a lunge,' he wrote, 'and I guess they were about right.'

We could do with more of his kind to enliven the scene today. Long live the swayers, lungers and bashers, I say! They put hope into the hearts of us all.

[1] I need hardly add that experts of today, like Palmer and Nicklaus, are models of decorum and discretion, presenting a fine public image of the professional golfer.

Golftopia

My comments on the virtues of the small canvas drainpipe golf bag as against the trolley brought a volume of support as gratifying as it was surprising, together with numerous suggestions for a tie for the society to be formed among those of us who carry this antiquated form of equipment.

On the other hand it has to be confessed that views were that I (*a*) was trying to do honest men out of a living, and (*b*) must have had a liver when I wrote it—one of which could have been true but wasn't; the other, never. Others suggested that it was time I stopped living in the past.

Well, sometimes the past has something to contribute to the present. Some things are better than they were and others were better than they are. It all set me wondering. Given the general conception of golf, which is now played by more grown-ups than any other game in the world, what would be the ideal conditions under which we should play if we could begin all over again?

We each have our own ideas of Golftopia and these are mine. I see a course ranging, according to the tees, from 6,000 to 6,200 yards (the present championship courses average about 7,000, plus 1,200 yards of walking between green and tee). This will include four short holes, two very long ones, one or two drive-and-a-pitch, and several where the second shot calls for a wooden club or 2-iron.

The short holes will face the four points of the compass and one of them will be very short indeed.

Like every other hole, however, it will conform to the principle that the size of the target varies in ratio to the size of the shot, and the green will therefore be microscopic. This will apply also to the long holes since, at about 480 yards, they will be out of range of two shots and the third will be only a pitch—provided you have hit the first two. If not, you will be hard put to it to get a five.

For the long handicap player, the beginner and the elderly, there will be no bunkers into which they can drive. These will be reserved for the longer and more skilful, and will be placed diagonally and with devilish ingenuity, tempting them to bite off as much as they think they can chew.

We shall have three tees in permanent use at each hole, the middle one within a few yards of the previous green; there will be several alternative starting points, and the eighteenth green will be under the club-house windows. As a consolation to those who are temporarily off their game, the course will enjoy magnificent views and an abundance of wild life.

Since it is easier (though this has not dawned in the last twenty years) to fit one ball to 1,500 courses than to alter 1,500 courses to fit one ball, we shall have a ball which the local scratch player can hit about 220 yards from the tee on a fine spring day. Perhaps Dr. Barnes Wallis, of 'Dam Buster' fame, who I see has invented a new cricket ball, can help us on this before frustration causes him to emigrate.

The club-house will be unpretentious, rural in aspect, and something between the original tin shed and the converted mansion—an old farmhouse maybe. No other dwelling-place will be visible from it, and from the veranda we shall be able to venture a modest wager on our friends performing on a practice putting course of superlative excellence, enclosed by rambler roses.

Within, there will be a small and somewhat austere men's bar, but elsewhere and on the course women will have equal rights, except when it is inconvenient for the men for them to do so. In the main rooms, at any rate at week-ends, the drinks will be laid out on a side table, and everyone will help themselves, putting the money in a pudding basin provided for the purpose with the same punctilious exactitude that they accord to an absent news-vendor when buying their evening paper.

Lunch will consist of one hot dish—after all, we don't get a choice at home—and a number of cold things on the side, including blue Cheshire cheese and a host of salads and vegetables grown in the steward's garden without the aid of chemical fertilizers.

It will be a tradition of the club that you can come up without a game and always be sure of getting one; that four-somes will be played on Sunday afternoons; and that the members not only patronize the professional's shop, but frequently invite him to play. Innumerable small boys will, of course, be on hand to carry our clubs.

There will be no annual subscription. At the end of the year the hon. secretary will inform each of our 100-odd members how much he owes. I hope that it will not, as happened in an American club of my acquaintance, come to $5,000 a head, but what if it does? With income tax at ninepence in the pound we shall be able to afford our Golftopia.

Sitting Pretty

Whatever Gilbert and Sullivan may have said about the policeman's lot, I cannot help feeling that that of the professional golfer today has its compensations.

After the rigours of the British Open Championship, which —though it comes in the first week of July and will, so the championship committee declare, continue to do so—is in a sense the climax of the season, the touring professionals from Britain, Australia, South Africa, Eire, and the golfing countries of Europe move agreeably and economically to the championships of Belgium, France, Holland and Germany.

At the moment the caravan is resting in the sunshine here at St. Germain, preparing for the first round of the oldest and perhaps the greatest of the European open championships, which begins tomorrow.

The French Open was first played in 1906 and for the first two years was won by Arnaud Massy. Now the massive trophy bears on its silver base many of the most distinguished names in golf—Taylor, Braid, Duncan, Hagen, Tolley, Whitcombe, Cotton, Locke and Nelson. Here is something worth winning for glory as well as francs.

Norman von Nida, with whom I walked round, was the centre of attraction this morning. His tempestuous days left far behind him, Von Nida is now a sort of elder statesman-cum-adviser among the young Commonwealth professionals.

I have to confess, however, that it was neither this nor the fact that he was playing round with that pair so familiar to British viewers, Thomson and Thomas, that drew all eyes in his direction. It was his caddy.

Long golden curls cascaded over her shoulders, and she wears a little red blouse and abbreviated blue trousers. I have been working out that she is too young to be the daughter and too old to be the grand-daughter of the one who caddied for Eric Martin Smith here in the Amateur Championship in 1929 and so greatly disturbed the members of the Cambridge University team of that year.

Von Nida serves as a sort of universal provider of golf clubs for his young followers. He has now gone through the best part of four sets, which are theoretically out on loan but which, like books, are not expected to return.

In addition, he has distributed about eight putters, with one of which, Von Nida, having cajoled it out of a fellow professional for £15, Thomson won the Open. It seemed a commonplace upright hickory shafted affair to me, but handsome is as handsome does.

Also out of Von Nida's bag—though in this case it was only returning to its original owner—came the driver with which Thomson won at Lytham. This is what he calls his 'soft' driver—and so indeed it seemed when I waggled it. It has plenty of loft, and it struck me that most members of the Curtis Cup team could swing it with ease.

On looking at Lytham in its uncharacteristically short and lush condition, Thomson said he at once decided that what was wanted was not length but direction. With his 'hard' driver, which has a stiff shaft and practically no loft, he could have got 20 yards further, but might in four rounds have hit four into the rough and lost four strokes.

This seemed to support a widely held belief that the older we get the more most of us would benefit from playing with lighter clubs. It sent my mind back to the long driving competitions before the German Open two years ago, when it came to the turn of that mighty hitter, Jean Baptiste Ado, to strike off from the elevated 18th tee at Frankfurt. Down on the fairway we all moved respectfully back about 40 yards, but a moment later everyone was ducking for safety as Ado's first ball pitched among the crowd. Later it transpired that, having mislaid his own, he had borrowed a woman's driver. It seemed like a matchstick in his hand.

This borrowing of clubs strikes me as rather refreshing, and I am glad to know that it still goes on. In the old days it was the normal thing to add clubs as you went along, and I believe I am right in saying that Walter Travis not only borrowed the famous Schenectady putter with which he won the Amateur Championship of 1904, but also added a new club from the professional's shop before every round.

Another of Thomson's reflections on Lytham which may, I think, be of general interest was that he said he had 'never seen such beautiful sand'. Lytham has, I believe, about 200 bunkers, and the modern professional hopes, of course, that if he does not finish on the green he will finish in one of them, when he can 'splash' it out with certainty and ease, rather than in some more hazardous grassy bank or hollow.

Thomson also suggested that, while the help of these enthusiastic ladies is much appreciated, the services of markers in championships are in fact superfluous and fewer unfortunate errors would be made if players marked each other's scores.

On the eve of the championship on this lovely course outside Paris, all in a sense are sitting pretty, but one is sitting prettier than most.

The other day the dapper little Italian professional, Angelini, was playing at Villa D'Este with a royal personage who is one of the most enthusiastic golfers in Europe. 'What is the record for this course?' the lady asked. 'Sixty-two,' he replied. 'Sixty-two!' she said. 'If *you* go round in 62, I will give you an Alfa Romeo.' Angelini, driving cautiously with an iron at the last two holes, finished in 62.

Next day a man called on him. 'I have come to inquire,' he said, 'what colour you would like it.'

Ancient and Modern

An hour or two ago we tee-ed off, so to speak, under the outstretched wings of the Liver birds—as in 'fiver', I need hardly say, not as in 'liver'—which preside over the Cunard dock at Liverpool.

Now the Blackpool Tower, bringing back memories of the two names Thomson and Thomas, with which the Open Championship of 1958 will ever be associated, has slipped astern on the right and, as we stop to drop the pilot, the Great Orme and Llandudno gleam in the distant evening sun on the left. The good ship *Sylvania* steams steadily on.

Perhaps she is successor to the ultimately torpedoed *Transsylvania* on which the British Walker Cup team were reported by an American writer—can it really be twenty-two years ago?—to be 'moving slowly, almost imperceptibly towards our shores'. This time it is the Curtis Cup of which we are in pursuit, or perhaps I should say the Americans are in pursuit of it, for of the three trophies for which we play them we are at the moment in possession of two, and this is one of them.

I find my thoughts alternating between the ancient and the ultra-modern. We are approaching the land of the electric caddie cart and the $4\frac{1}{2}$-hour round, where no fewer than five million dedicated golfers, headed by their President, pursue their way round 5,000 courses, counting every stroke at every hole. Yet my mind has been turning to the past, rather than the future, to the dim distant figure of W. T. Linskill, who in 1875, together with a few friends, was the founder of Cambridge University golf.

Not long ago I was presented at St. Andrews with a handsome, twin-handled, glass-bottomed pewter tankard bearing the legend 'Cambridge University Golf Club. 3rd prize for Scratch score. Won by W. T. Linskill, March, 1877'. I hope on my return to present it in turn to the University club. However, it was followed almost at once by another reader sending me *Golf* by W. T. Linskill, published in the All-England series, price 1s., in 1889—and a most intriguing travelling companion it has proved.

How do you pronounce golf? Personally I have always called it golf—or tried to. Goalf may be ruled out as an abomination on a par with trousers tucked into the socks. To my surprise, however, Linskill is in no doubt on the matter. 'The term "golf", pronounced "goff",' he says in his opening sentence, 'is evidently derived from the German. . . .' Senior readers may be able to enlighten us. Was 'goff' really the U-word when the game spread to England? And, if so, when did it become non-U, which it surely is now?

'Goff' I can believe, but can it really be that Linskill and the founders of Cambridge golf talked of putters to rhyme with footer? Yet there is evidence that they may well have done. After talking of fancy putters—'some with double faces, others as swans with curled necks, and some even fashioned in the shape of a mallet'—he dismissed them as monstrosities and says that no amount of eccentric instruments will make a bad 'putter' 'put' better. Again, he defines the club itself as the one used for 'putting' the ball into the hole. Did footing the bill and putting the ball really sound the same in Linskill's day?

I like the qualities he outlines as desirable for the devotee of the new up-and-coming game. A good golfer, he says, should possess 'the cool head of a professional whist or chess player, the arms of a navvy or blacksmith, and the untiring energy of a devoted September sportsman'. His dress will comprise 'a loose coat; a loose shirt with no stiffened abominations such as front, collars and cuffs; well-nailed boots; and no braces, but instead thereof a waistbelt so that there may be no impediment to a perfect freedom of action'.

This last seems quite dogmatic, yet I distinctly remember having been told a story once of James Braid having lost an open championship through mislaying—or bursting, I forget which—his braces and being unable to play without them.

Here is another thing that intrigues me. After outlining for possible recruits the many virtues of golf, he is at great pains to convince them that it is not so 'dangerous' a game as it has been painted. 'Indeed,' he says, 'in the whole course of my experience I have been struck only three times.' Twice it was by spent balls and once 'through the carelessness of a stupid and inexperienced caddie on the Cambridge links.'

Linskill at the time of writing had been playing for eighteen years. How many of us, playing on the crowded courses of today, could say lightly that we had 'been struck only three times'? Personally in exactly twice that period I have not yet, touch wood, been struck at all, and only once to my knowledge have struck another—and he, on coming out of hospital, sold me a golfer's insurance policy!

What a far cry it is from those days when Linskill was laying out, and winning pewter tankards, upon the muddy patch at Coldham Common, near Cambridge—the worst course, so I am always assured, in all the length and breadth of Merrie England! Now, lady golfers fly the Atlantic to do battle with Americans, the amateurs of thirty nations are soon to assemble in friendly combat for the Eisenhower Trophy at St. Andrews, and the professionals for the Canada Cup at Mexico City, because it is 'more central'. I wonder what he would have thought of it all?

Bitter Pills

How strange are the lapses of human memory—and none more strange than those suffered by people who play, attempt to play, or watch the game of golf.

Among the many dramatic incidents, for instance, upon which Bobby Jones may look back, none can be stamped more indelibly on his mind than the occasion on which, during his first visit to this country as a very young man, he tempestuously tore up his card at the short eleventh hole at St. Andrews. It is an episode which has been quoted and re-quoted ever since.

He told of it in detail at the unbelievably moving ceremony at which he was presented with the freedom of the Royal Borough. He recalled how he had driven into the Hill bunker, taken two or three to get out, gone over the green into the little bunker at the back where the ground slopes sharply down to the Eden Estuary, taken two more in there—and torn up.

Now the fact is that within the memory of the oldest inhabitant, and indeed almost for a certainty within the 400 years during which golf has been played on the links of St. Andrews, there has never been a bunker behind the eleventh green. Jones himself freely accepts this. 'Nevertheless,' he said, 'I never took two shots in a bunker and failed to remember it yet!'

In 1926 Jones played another historic bunker shot—175 yards to the seventeenth green at Lytham—which won him the Open from Al Watrous, with whom he was partnered and was at that time level. This bunker is one of a series of sand traps, and a few years ago the members of Lytham erected a sort of 'tombstone' therein to commemorate his feat. Hundreds of people witnessed the stroke, but there remain to this day many who declare with hand on heart that the tombstone is in the wrong bunker.[1]

Among them is Mr. Norman Doley, of Cooden Beach, with whom I was talking in the train on the way home. As Jones's ball flew, incredibly, to the heart of the green, he happened, he said, to be standing beside Watrous. 'There,' said Watrous, visibly shaken, 'goes $100,000!' And so indeed it proved.

A few minutes later Walter Hagen came to the final hole, needing a two to tie, and sent his caddie forward to hold the flag. Referring to this some time ago, I recounted, though I was not, of course, there, how his ball had missed the flag by inches and finished in the geraniums under the clubhouse windows. I was at once corrected.

It wasn't geraniums, said members who had been there at the time. It was a bunker. Though the bunker has now gone, they said, there was never at any time a flower bed at the back of the eighteenth. Others who were also present rallied to my support. Nonsense, they said. They could see Hagen to this day, hitting it out of the geraniums.

This fallibility of golfing memory extends itself to one's own play. There is an old story of the man who, on being asked how he had got on, replied that he had been off his game, and then added, 'Come to think of it, I am never *on*

---

[1] Two correspondents wrote to say that they were standing next to Jones when he played this historic shot and that he was not in sand at all but in rough grass between two bunkers.

my game.' Yet all of us have moments, however fleeting, when everything goes right at once and we are 'on'. One would think that one could remember, possibly for as much as twenty-four hours, the elementary details of stance, grip and backswing, and possibly some single 'secret' that brought about this happy state.

How many people, I wonder, on the basis that the only way to remember a dream is to write it down at the time, have resorted to the diagrams and memoranda? Certainly I have myself. If so, we are in good company, for I even seem to remember some years ago, if he will pardon the disclosure, Mr. Cyril Tolley consulting some hieroglyphics which he carried about with him under the elastic band in his cigarette case. I can see him doing it. But perhaps, after all, it was Mr. T. A. Torrance.

My own tribulations in this respect, though of little public interest, may yet strike a sympathetic chord. Caught in the situation, familiar to every dedicated golfer, of being, in the late Mrs. Zaharias's brilliant phrase, 'fouled up in the mechanics of the game', I have been straightened out, de-straightened, and re-straightened by sundry distinguished advisers, not excluding Cotton.

As I had sliced for thirty years, he said that the only thing, especially as our figures were not dissimilar, was to stand like Locke—i.e. aiming at cover-point, twisting round on the backswing till you are aiming direct at point, and proceeding from there. Then however much you heave round to the left as you come down, you are still hitting 'from the inside'.

This was tried, and towards the end of the second bucket of balls at the golf school a compromise between the Locke and the orthodox brought the desired result. Drive after drive flew painlessly into the distance as though fired from a rifle. The magic stance—distance from ball, position of feet, angle of approach, and so on—was measured and committed earnestly to memory.

The next day brought two bitter pills to swallow. Not only, as you may imagine, had I forgotten the formula and reverted to type, but I, the proud owner of the Clayton windmills known as Jack and Jill, failed to notice that Jack and Jill, ridden by Clayton, was running at Ascot. It won, while my back was turned, at 20–1.

Tomorrow will do

As I sit on the terrace at Madrid airport basking in the balmy sunshine and no longer bothering as to when the plane, already delayed an hour, will leave, or when anyone will be given any further information about it, in a language which none of us in any case can understand, I reflect that a short sojourn in Spain does the English a great deal of good. It is a splendid corrective to the hustle and bustle on which, under the guise of efficiency, we nowadays set such store.

Some of the party, it is true, did not quite have time to assimilate the lesson that tomorrow will do just as well as today, and I retain a lively memory of the scene as our group of assorted professional golfers and camp followers endeavoured to extricate themselves from the hotel, some indulging in a tug-of-war with the enraged concierge for possession of their clubs, for which it appeared they had not acquired a 'baggage clearance', others yelling at them from the bus that we had only minutes to spare if all were to catch their respective aeroplanes.

The gesticulations and general commotion attracted a crowd almost as big as that which had turned out to see the match for the Joy Cup, and in the end we drove off in triumph to the strains of the theme tune from the film *The Bridge on the River Kwai*, for which the citizens of Madrid may be seen queueing from early morning onwards.

So here we are, sitting in the sunshine some hours later, certain in the knowledge that we shall get to Lisbon if and when the aeroplane gets there and not a moment before, so why worry? and with plenty of time to reflect on the match in which Britain have beaten the Rest of Europe and the scene in which they have done it.

One of my first impressions is that our leading players, now that they have added so many Continental events to their rota of competitions at home, may be in danger of allowing themselves to be turned into tournament professionals, instead of club professionals, as has happened in America to the detriment of both the game and the players. I think the present group may be thoroughly stale—through no fault of their own—and the sooner they are able to settle down for a while at their clubs the better.

Secondly, after seeing the magnificent course at the Club de Campo, it occurs to me that J. Arana, who used to play golf for Spain, must be one of the very best golf architects in the world today. He also laid out the course at Barcelona, which I have heard at least one competent judge describe as the finest seaside course in Europe.

The Club de Campo is a kind of Hurlingham or Roehampton on the grand scale—it has 5,000 members—with polo grounds, horse-jumping course, tennis courts and swimming pools, to say nothing of an engineering school where they train 60 caddies for productive jobs in later life.

The single-storey white club-house is perched on top of a hill from which one looks across to the entire city of Madrid on its plateau—four miles away but seeming, in the amazingly clear atmosphere, to be just across the valley.

Amid this rolling, greyish-brown, arid country, studded with olives and cypress trees and strangely reminiscent of Palestine, Arana has laid out a 7,000-yard course, comparable in at least one way with Pine Valley in that there is no semi-rough. You are either on an island of vivid green fairway or you are in among the trees.

No golfing visitor to Spain should pass near Madrid without a visit to this exceptional course. Across the valley is the other Madrid course, the Puerta de Hierro, a shorter and rather trickier eighteen holes laid out a few years ago by Mr. Tom Simpson. Between the two of them these courses must represent as fine a week-end golf as you will find in Europe.

The individual success of the present tour has been Peter Alliss. He did, it is true, lose his single by a narrow margin to A. Miguel, a familiar figure in British tournaments and the most accomplished player in Spain, but he won both the Spanish and Italian open championships by the fantastic margin of ten shots. Now, in Portugal, he will have a chance of completing an unprecedented treble.[1]

Incidentally, the British captain, Dai Rees, put Alliss to bring up the rear in the singles. It has been a common practice in international matches for some years—started, I fancy, by the Americans—to put a strong man at the end. I remember Snead, for instance, playing last in a Ryder Cup match. Yet I often wonder whether, instead of all the crafty juggling about, it would not be better to play the singles in all team matches—Walker, Ryder and Curtis Cups, internationals and the University match—in order of merit.

It has always seemed to me that anyone who was the best player of his day is entitled to tell his grandchildren 'I once played top for Britain'—or, in humbler spheres, 'I once played third for Lancashire', or ninth for Cambridge, or whatever it may be. Furthermore, if they want a strong man at the end then clearly the top players should go out last. What a splendid experiment this would be for the University match, when the leading singles often go off in comparative obscurity early in the morning and the very men who ought to be bearing the brunt of it themselves leave a desperate finish to be fought out by the trembling 'tail'.

However, that was a diversion—and now there comes another. Hasty shufflings indicate that we may at last be on the move. Next stop, with luck, Lisbon.

[1] He did. An open championship against the best in Britain and the Rest of Europe each Saturday for three weeks. A fantastic feat.

High Level Stuff

It is funny how single remarks stick in one's mind. A year
or so ago I was sitting in an aeroplane somewhere between
Tokyo and a hideous, aptly-named airstrip called Cold Bay
beside Mario Gonzales, whom followers of golf in this
country may remember as a pencil-thin young fellow playing
in the 1948 Amateur Championship at Sandwich and later
in the Open at Muirfield. In the following year he turned
professional and is now at the Santa Amare club, where his
father was professional before him, at São Paulo, Brazil.

Gonzales had been representing Brazil in the Canada Cup
tournament in Japan and was complaining that it was a
long, long way from home. He had been sitting upright in an
aeroplane for four days and nights on the way out, he said,
and now he had another three days and nights of it before he
got home. Japan, he thought, was too far away. 'Next year,'
he said, 'they ought to play it at Mexico City. It's more
central.' More central! To such a degree, I remember
thinking, has the aeroplane shrunk the circumference of the
globe. Now, in 1958, Gonzales's desire has come true and
Mexico City it is to be.

In a letter which Her Majesty's Ambassador, Sir Andrew
Noble, has been kind enough to write to me, asking in what
way he might entertain the British delegation without en-
dangering their training, he remarks that Mexico City is

7,500 feet above sea level 'but the ordinary man in good athletic training does not find this too much of a handicap'.

Thank you, sir, for the compliment but this cannot, unfortunately, be reconciled with other opinions. Only the other day Flory Van Donck, who is representing Belgium, was giving me awful warnings that no one should proceed to such an altitude without a doctor's certificate. This advice I have declined to take, partly on account of the difficulty in getting hold of the doctor but largely through apprehension of his verdict.

I recall that last year, during the same expedition that took me to Tokyo, I had the luck to play a round at Banff in Alberta, which must be scenically one of the most magnificent places in which golf is played. On the 1st tee, playing with three kindly and hospitable folk for a total liability of a dollar and a half, I felt rather as though I were engaged in the thirty-seventh hole of the final of the Amateur Championship. 'Ah,' they said, when at last my form seemed to call for some explanation, 'it's the altitude.' Banff, however, is only 4,500 ft.

It so happened that last week I found myself playing in a foursome with those intrepid wartime aviators, P. B. Lucas and Douglas Bader, and here surely would be the voice of authenticity. I was not encouraged. One of them assured me that he 'always made the boys turn on the oxygen before 7,000', and the other kept recounting some story about his athletic young friend in the prime of life who was setting out to play golf at La Paz, nipped back into the hotel to fetch his shoes—and passed flat out on the top step. I forget how long it took to bring him round.

*

The journey so far afield as Mexico leaves many impressions on the mind, not all of them related to the golf, which was strictly the object of the visit. Ireland brought the Canada Cup home and O'Connor played a splendid supporting role—but Harry Bradshaw was the hero.

I will not harp further on the difficulties of playing golf at high altitudes, but it will hardly be disputed that, weight for weight and age for age, they progressively increase.

On a course longer than any British championship links and with a strict par of 72, Bradshaw had rounds of 70, 70, 76 and 70—and he is forty-five and carries 15 stone. When others were sinking exhausted in the locker room, he was ready with affable conversation, and, as for the alleged danger of dysentery, 'I dhrink t'water out of t'tap. If you're going to get it, you'll get it anyway.'

A year ago in Tokyo, he had to retire from this tournament through persistent nose bleeding. I saw him standing cheerfully in the hotel entrance as we left. Only three or four people, of whom I was not one, then knew that in the intervening days he had been so near to death that a priest had been called to administer the last rites. My colleagues are due shortly to elect a Golfer of the Year who has 'done most for British Golf'. Had they seen him in Mexico, they would look no further than Harry Bradshaw—and never mind what part of Ireland he comes from!

The two golfing bees in my personal bonnet—the length of the golf ball and slowness of play—were exhibited in Mexico in such full and magnificent idiocy that I must wait for another day to do them justice.

Reverting from golf, I was not the only Englishman to sense that if ever there were an up-and-coming country it is Mexico and that, if I had a surplus million, I would at once invest it there. The caricature of Mexico is a thing of the past. The parade to celebrate the last revolution took two and a half hours to pass my window and was devoted almost wholly to the arts of physical prowess. Not a man or a girl can have been more than thirty, and a finer lot I never saw.

Furthermore, believe it or not, they like the British. I soon learnt that to slip into the conversation 'I come from London'—as opposed, I fear, to Texas or New York—was the 'open sesame' to gleaming smiles and enthusiastic handshakes. My heart naturally warmed in return—till they drove me in their motor-cars, when it sank to my boots. Their driving is based on the first principle of carmanship: 'The man who loses his nerve first goes across last.' Rather like playing 'nibs' at school, with the reverse object, namely, to ensure that the other fellow hits you amidships rather than vice-versa, thus proving himself in the wrong.

Of many crowded impressions the strongest is that of the journey home and here we may indeed be proud. Six hours direct from Mexico City to New York in the Britannia; six and a half hours direct from New York in the Comet. It is true that we landed on the wrong green, so to speak, and found ourselves breakfasting at Prestwick, but that was no fault of the Comet.

Doubtless it will become one day commonplace, but at the moment the Comet is not so much an aeroplane as an Experience. The Rolls-Royce engines, tucked in close beside the passengers' cabin, must be 25 feet long, and the surge of power as the machine takes off makes one feel extraordinary small. I remember in particular as it soared steeply into the sky a stewardess positively heaving herself up from one seat-back to the next as she tried to make her way to the forward cabin.

Up aloft, alone in the firmament at 40,000 ft., one sits for some hours apparently stationary. One can balance a penny on the table, the liquid in one's glass does not even tremble, and the only item of equipment missing is the billiard table.

And how right psychologically were De Havillands in insisting that their men take care not to scratch the Comet's glistening outer sheath. All other aeroplanes look tatty by comparison. I even felt affronted when someone refuelling at Prestwick left rubber sole marks on the wing outside my window.

We ended in a 'stack'—somewhere over Watford the captain said—circling for half an hour in a world of our own: shirt-sleeves, dark glasses, the sun blazing down on a limit-less waste of cotton wool stretching away to a curved horizon. Not alone this time but with half a dozen others.

One by one their turn came to disappear below, and eventually ours. The sun went in, the fog swirled, and out we came, just over the hangars of London Airport into the grey world in which it is our lot for so many months to live.

How tantalizing to think that all the time that other world is only a few thousand feet above our heads. Dammit, I'd rather be stacked over Watford!

Gifted Amateur

In the present conforming society when several million citizens may at any one moment be glued to the same commercial on the telly, the company of a nonconformist is always to be relished. One such is, and has always been, Tom Simpson, best known for his work as a golf architect, though in fact a connoisseur of life in general. The other day in a letter to a mutual friend he was regretting the fact that he would not see his obituary, as penned by your correspondent.

Knowing how strongly it would appeal to that love of the unconventional which has made him the bane of so many golf club committees in his fifty years of designing golf courses, I suggested repairing the omission, so to speak, in advance. '*De mortuis*,' it is said, '*Nil nisi bonum*.' In the present instance I have the victim's cheerful invitation to write anything I —— well please, and a guaranteed immunity from writs.

In eighty-two years Tom Simpson has touched life at an enviable number of points and I have always attributed to this fact his refusal to produce for golfing clients anything which he himself deemed humdrum, however much they might desire it—as they often did. Indeed, I dare say that golf clubs in Britain have spent more money in undoing his work than that of all the other architects put together.

The 'grooved-swing' golfer of today abhors the element of

luck and anything in the shape of an intelligence test. Tom Simpson with the utmost relish gave them both.

His life has been one of unwavering hostility towards government by committees in any shape or form and of ceaseless endeavour to get 'one up' on them. His first move when invited to construct or alter a course was to win the first hole by turning up in a Rolls-Royce. It thus became tacitly understood from the start that, if they did not like the result of his labours, they could do the other thing. This occurred at Sunningdale in connection with the New course, on which he set a particularly fierce examination to the powerful player. The conventionalized version by which at such expense it was replaced has been done, doubtless to his delight, in 63.

His outstanding work, the monuments by which he will long be remembered, are on the Continent and in Southern Ireland, where he found his way of thinking more in tune with that of the customer. They include, among my personal acquaintance, Spa and Royal Antwerp in Belgium; in Eire those two magnificent courses, Ballybunion and Baltray; and Morfontaine, surely the finest inland course in France, where I once had the pleasure, on hearing him say rather airily 'Where's the 1st tee here?' of replying: 'The same place that you put it in twenty-five years ago'. Anyone with such a coterie of courses to his credit—and there are, of course, many more than those I have quoted—deserves to be heard with respect, if not always with agreement.

Among Mr. Simpson's views are, for instance, that the Old course at St. Andrews stands out incomparably from all others, and that the thirteenth is the best single hole in golf. He claims that in fifty years he has never set a bunker to catch a bad shot—which, on a well designed course, should create its own punishment—but only to catch the not-quite-good-enough shot of the good player. On one Scottish course he found 1,300 bunkers, He left it with 65.

'No course can be truly great without an out-of-bounds,' is another of his maxims. 'Then I take it you regard Hoylake as the best in England?' I remember saying. 'Without any doubt whatever,' was the reply. And, inland, Liphook and Woking in that order—Liphook only 6,000-odd yards, and 70 broken only once in thirty-five years.

Would he like to go back to Ye Olde Golfe and the guttie? 'Certainly not. I would never have allowed the rubber-cored ball in the first place—but not one person in fifty who plays today would want to play with a guttie.' What would he like to do then? 'Adopt the American ball. Ban the wedge. And halve the number of clubs.'

Some of Tom Simpson's views may sound reactionary to younger golfers, who never knew the more diversified art of golf in the days when clubs were known by names instead of numbers; but they are those of an artist in life as well as in golf.

He has published a most beautiful book on contemporary etchings, is a painter of no mean talent, and was for some time art critic of *The Saturday Review*, whose editor employed him 'not because of his writing, which was often deplorable, but because he wrote with knowledge and conviction'.

He has collected wines, walking sticks, Persian rugs, eighteenth-century furniture, and cigars, of which at a conservative estimate he has smoked 45,000, but perhaps his most unexpected talent has been in making needlework pictures of golf holes in *petit-point*. I saw only the other day a picture he had done of the eighth hole at Cruden Bay, 600 stitches to the square inch and ten or a dozen shades of wool blended together to portray the heather and bracken. It was quite wonderful.

Taken by and large, Tom Simpson has been one of those lucky few who never really 'turned pro'. He remains the gifted amateur. It occurs to me that we could do with more of his kind today.

What a Man!

If a boy delights in lying on his back between the rails at night for the pleasure of watching express trains run over him and can later claim to have been birched more times in a given period than any other Etonian, it may be taken as likely that he will grow up to be something of a 'character'. This was certainly true of Sir Raymond Quilter, and the world is much, much the poorer for his loss.

Versatile and eccentric, inventive yet extremely practical, he must have packed a greater variety of experience into his fifty-six years than most men would contrive if they had their lives half a dozen times over again.

I met him first in connection with golf, which was in a sense the only one of his abiding interests which ever defeated him. He attacked it with tremendous vigour and saw no reason why, with a few intelligent modifications here and there, it should not, like anything else, be made to work. He easily got down to scratch, of course, but despite a succession of short cuts, hints, tips, new sets of clubs, and hundreds of hours of practice, the ultimate secret evaded him. It was almost the only one that did.

When he left Eton, Quilter went as a 'probationer' into the Grenadiers, where, strangely one would have thought, he decided he could improve the technique of high-speed cycling. He was riding, head down and flat out, round the square at Windsor when he ran into a cannon. A brother officer who helped to carry him to hospital recalls that his life was despaired of. In the early hours of the morning he 'came to' and was heard practising on a saxophone. This was confiscated by the M.O.

In this period he began what was to be the principal serious work of his life, destined to save hundreds of lives and to be rewarded, exceptionally, by the Air Ministry, by an *ex gratia* payment of £27,000. At the Household Brigade Flying Club's meeting at Hanworth in the late 'twenties he made a parachute descent.

Now that he could no longer lie under trains, here was the perfect substitute. He made incessant descents, trying out new parachutes of his own design, often delaying their opening till his friends had given him up for lost. One of them told me that one day he had disappeared behind the level of the neighbouring trees with the parachute still unopened. He pitched in a rock garden in Weybridge and 'broke his leg like a pistol shot'.

For some time he instructed in the art at Brooklands. His account of these days remains vividly in my memory. You got the victim out on the wing and at the appropriate moment seized his wrist and flung him clear. He never forgot to pull the ring. Some, however, 'knew all the answers'. There was nothing to it. In this case Quilter would signal to the pupil to jump at the precise moment calculated to lower him slowly but inexorably into the adjacent sewage farm.

He turned his genius towards dropping loads heavier than man. I wonder if we number among our readers the air crew adrift in the Bay of Biscay to whom a Sunderland from Plymouth dropped a motorboat (in which they drove themselves back to England) with eight huge parachutes. These were Quilter's. So were the ones with which, at Ringway in 1942, they dropped heavy containers from 8,000 feet, with the parachutes calculated to open at 250 feet. The device worked and there are those who will declare that if it had not been 'sat on' for two years it could have saved the troops at Arnhem.

Later he bought John Cobb's Napier-Railton to test brake-parachutes on the runway at Dunsfold, where there was just room to get it up to 120 m.p.h. before, if he or the parachute did not brake, they would go through the hedge.

As a substitute for normal sport during the war, Quilter took up bomb disposal. Another of his 'lines' was designing diving-suits, in which he naturally played the main experimental role himself. I would give much to have been present when under an East Coast pier he tugged at a fisherman's line and amid unparalleled excitement was 'played' for some minutes before revealing himself.

What a life he had! He was a tremendous shot—a natural follow-on from the catapult days at Eton—but to make it more difficult decided to, and did, master the bow and arrow. His steel bows were wicked affairs. He shot rabbits with them and could hit a handkerchief at 60 yards.

He possessed a library that any man might envy, was undoubtedly one of the finest cooks in London, and was a photographer—with every latest gadget of course—of outstanding ability.

He was one of the three people whom I would class as the best company I have ever known. No one can have brought a more instant enlivenment to the party by his arrival or reduced more people to actual tears of laughter. In its way it is a tribute to the humble game of golf that it should have been the only thing to beat him.

Guns or Putter

Some months ago it came to my knowledge that a friend of mine, Captain Quentin Paterson, R.N., a naval gunnery expert now retired, had been observed firing golf balls at Huntercombe.

There were tales of missiles crashing in the wood beside startled players on the seventeenth green, fired from the tee 400 yards away. Inquiry proved, however, that the apparatus was not yet perfected, and so indeed it seemed when the Captain let off a salvo from the steps of the Royal and Ancient during the Eisenhower Trophy week.

While he could undoubtedly outdrive any man present and several times carried the Swilcan Burn 370 yards away, one shot was so far off course as to pitch on the ladies' putting green, 60 yards adrift. For a man who, on being seconded to industry, had built 16-inch guns which could 'guarantee to hit a tennis court six times out of eight at 12 miles', this was far from satisfactory.

He thought at first that he was up against the same problem of swerve that baffled eighteenth-century gunners and was proved by the Germans in 1840 to be due to the centre of gravity of a spherical missile not always being in its geometrical centre. The true answer, however, turned out to be spin. By projecting a shallow rib over the end of the muzzle he was able to catch the ball on its way out and set it back-spinning, as it does when hit with a golf club. The time was thus ripe for a long promised private demonstration.

The weapon is a Very pistol with a barrel 18 inches long and a bore of 1·622 inches (the British ball being 1·62). He had fired his first shot with a 12-bore cartridge and the ball flew out so fast that he never saw it. It was later recovered by chance 800 yards away. He therefore reduced the charge from 23 grains of nitro to 7½ of black powder, which is much less powerful than nitro, loaded in a shortened ·410 cartridge case. This 7½ grains is no more, in bulk, than you get in a 6d. packet of antirrhinum seed and, when touched off with a match, goes up with a pleasing flash and a barely audible 'poof'. Incredibly, this tiny amount will send a golf ball 240 yards.

The effect with and without the 'spin-brake' proved to be most revealing. Without it a ball aimed horizontally hit the ground 20 yards away; with it, 200 yards. Aimed with elevation the figures were 150 and 250. In performing its function the spin-brake is liable to break the ball's cover in two places. The captain cheerfully cuts off the raised bit with a penknife, exposing the elastic within, and finds—if the golf ball makers will forgive my revealing it—that this makes no difference to the ball's subsequent flight whatever!

Our first shot with a very old ball was probably the most perfect played in Britain that day—about 300 yards dead into the wind and not veering an inch either way. The next was a new ball, which slipped down the barrel without touching the sides. (Older balls of another make had sometimes to be rammed down with some force. Does the ball increase in size, therefore, after being used?) At any rate, the new ball had just enough hook to take it into the bushes, whence it has doubtless been retrieved by one of the many private packs of ball-hunting hounds which operate at Huntercombe. Perhaps its centre of gravity was amiss. We shall never know.

The Captain's theories of spin, however, seemed abundantly proved. With the brake adjusted just to the left of centre the gun hooked; to the right it sliced. I then induced him to double the charge to 15 grains and see if we could drive the green, 421 yards into a freshening wind. The result was a tremendous, high, towering slice—a stroke with which on a much reduced scale I am only too familiar. It pitched, for those who know Huntercombe, just short of the bushes round the 2nd tee, the best part of 400 yards.

Paterson's Golf Gun (Patent pending) may prove of serious significance in solving many golf ball problems, including the eternal question of finding one which curbs the very long hitter without handicapping the short, though he himself has no answer to that one yet. In the meantime with two clubs, gun and putter, and a pocket full of selected charges ranging from 600 yards to 50, he reckons he is now almost in a position to take on the Open Champion.

His choice of club will at least be simple—a variation on the old theme—'Guns or Butter'. And when he gets in, we shall at least be yielding nothing to American parlance when we inquire 'How many did you shoot?'

Sharp Practice

As a rabid fan of my colleague, Ian Fleming, and James Bond, I am naturally delighted to find that in the latest episode the second of the latter's three skirmishes with the villainous Mr. Goldfinger takes place on the golf course. Furthermore, those who know Royal St. Georges—professional, Albert Whiting, short sixth hole known as the Maiden—will have little difficulty in following the play at Mr. Fleming's Royal St. Marks, Sandwich, where the professional is Alfred Blacking and the short sixth is known as the Virgin.

Mr. Goldfinger, as might be suspected of a man with creases down the sides of his plus-fours, cheats. I will not reveal the subterfuge whereby Bond outcheats him at the eighteenth,[1] but will say that the account of the match adds materially to the fictional literature of golf and sheds light

[1] In fact, though both Goldfinger and Bond had cheated outrageously at the seventeenth, Goldfinger did not, according to the Rules of Golf, cheat at the eighteenth. Bond 'called' him for doing so and took him for $10,000. I always think that it was more to Bond's credit to make Goldfinger cough up for infringing the Rules when he wasn't, than it would have been if he had. The truth is that with 93 pages of the Rules, to say nothing of heaven knows how many Decisions upon them, neither Bond, Goldfinger, nor Fleming—nor, if I may class myself with so distinguished a trio, myself—know them.

on an aspect of the game which has always fascinated me and on which I have often thought one day to write one of Sherlock Holmes's 'trifling monographs'.

Cheating at golf, like cheating at patience, is mostly so pointless as to have something rather splendid about it. There are, of course, exceptions, when there is very considerable point in it. Probably the outstanding example in the game's history was the singular incident in what we should call a selling sweep at a highly respectable American club some years ago, when a Mr. A, handicap 17, and Mr. B, handicap 18, made a net return of 58 and 57, a total of 115 for 36 holes.

This notable score won for the talented pair and the man who had bought them in the sweep some $16,000. Inquiry revealed, however, that Mr. A's handicap was not 17 but three and that Mr. B was not in fact Mr. B at all, but a young Mr. C, also handicap three, whom Mr. A had invited to come along and play under Mr. B's name and handicap. [On second thoughts I am not at all sure that Mr. A was in fact Mr. A either.]

Money is, of course, the root of nearly all major cheating at golf and nearly always the caddie is suborned into being an accomplice. I knew one club where too much money was habitually played for by people too keen to win it and most of the caddies were reckoned—though I personally did not have occasion to prove it—to have holes in their trouser pockets and a spare ball with the same identification marks as the one for which they were searching.

In warmer climates barefooted Negro caddies are tremendous manipulators of a golf ball with the big toe while gazing heavenwards with an air of saintly innocence. I also remember on one of the Hong Kong courses just after the war being accompanied by about half a dozen diminutive self-appointed fore-caddies who scuttled about in the rough ahead. It was not, I think, wholly coincidental that I inevitably got a fortunate lie.

Nor can I forbear mentioning yet again the late 'Wash' Carr's story of his driving far up the fairway at Walton Heath in a friendly match and finding his ball deep in a divot mark.

'That'd be a nice one to get in the Medal,' he said—to which the man replied darkly: 'You'd never 'ave 'ad it in the Medal.'

I like, too, the reply of another London golfer when playing in a Continental championship. He had driven into the rough and, after trying one or two clubs to see if he could get at the ball with them, eventually hacked it out with a niblick. His youthful opponent made some observation which he took to be suggestive, whereupon he retorted: 'Look here, young fellow, if I want to cheat, I start with the niblick and work up to the brassie!'

Women golfers, I am often assured, cheat nearly all the time, but I suspect that this may be the sort of unfair generalization that is usually levelled against women motorists. When you see a particularly abominable piece of driving by a man, you tend to say 'Look at that fellow'. If it is a woman, you say, 'These women!' Perhaps it would be fair to say that women in ordinary day-to-day golf do not adhere quite so meticulously to the rules—which is, of course, quite a different thing.

Far and away my favourite story is of a former Cambridge player, now dead, who really did cheat flagrantly and was known to do so. He was playing with Dale Bourn in the foursomes against a very well-known London club—I never go there without thinking of it—and at the last hole Dale drove into the bunker on the right, while the club pair were over to the left. Dale arrived in time to find his partner busily teeing up the ball in the bunker.

'I say. Look here,' he said, or words to that effect. His partner looked up. 'What?' he said. 'They didn't see me, did they?'

Law of the Links

'By special request' as the entertainers say when they have every intention of doing an encore anyway, I venture to produce an abbreviated set of golfing Rules which I feel might cover the day-to-day activities of club golfers who require a common code and have no intention of cheating. No more is claimed for it than that, but it might, when its various inadequacies have been pointed out and corrected, serve as a basis of an official abbreviated version to replace the 93 pages of the present pocket edition.[1]

It would be idle to deny that most people at the moment have only the sketchiest knowledge of the Rules. Those that follow could be printed—albeit in pretty small type—on the outside portions of a scorecard and everyone could reasonably be expected to be acquainted with them. For professionals playing for thousands of pounds it might be desirable to produce a sterner and more detailed code. If so, I have no doubt that the Rules of Golf Committee would give them a hand in doing so.

[1] Following—I will not say 'as a result of'—this article Mr. Gerald Micklem, at the moment of writing Chairman of the Rules of Golf Committee, produced for the Golf Foundation a short summary, of scorecard size, entitled 'Some Guidance to the Rules of Golf'. These are free to golf clubs in any quantity and about a hundred thousand have been distributed.

Local rules such as picking out of specified streams, burns, etc., under penalty of one stroke, and improving the lie (but not the stance) between, say, 1 November and 1 May would remain the concern of individual clubs.

Perhaps I may note certain points in the suggested Rules? There is, for instance, no limitation of clubs. Only in this way, it seems to me, can we hope to break down the absurd notion that a 'set' of golf clubs numbers fourteen. 'A 'set' is the number you choose to carry and would in most cases range from seven to nine. Again, I think that many minor contingencies, e.g. finding your ball on the wrong green or having a dog run off with it, would be covered, for club golfers at any rate, either by Rule 2 or by the words 'in the traditional manner' in Rule 1. I envisage that the 'background', i.e. form of clubs, amateur status, how to run a competition, etc., would remain available in a separate publication.

So here with due humility I set up to be shot at my plain man's Law of the Links:

1. The game shall be played in the traditional manner and with as little delay as possible. Penalty: match play, loss of hole. Stroke play, two strokes.

2. If any point in dispute be not covered by the Rules, it shall be settled in accordance with equity.

3. Ball lost, out of bounds or unplayable. The player may drop a ball on the nearest edge of the fairway under penalty of two strokes. Alternatively he may forthwith, under penalty of stroke and distance, play another ball from the same place as the first, the second ball then becoming the ball in play irrespective of where the first be later found.

4. Impediments and obstructions. Without penalty (1) any loose impediment may be removed, (2) a ball (a) in any hole, mark or matter left by an animal, (b) within two clubs' length of any artificial obstruction, (c) interfered with by anything left by the green-keeper, (d) lying on ground under repair or in sufficient casual

water to interfere with stroke or stance, may be dropped, or if necessary placed, clear.

5. A ball embedded in its pitch anywhere except in a sand bunker may be lifted and dropped without penalty.

6. On the green. The ball may be cleaned, pitch marks flattened and impediments scraped aside. No penalty shall be incurred for hitting the flagstick, whether attended or not, or for accidentally hitting partner, opponent, caddies or equipment. If a player's ball hit another, there shall be in match play no penalty, in stroke play a penalty of one stroke. The ball struck shall in all cases be replaced.

7. The nearer ball, anywhere on the course, shall be lifted at the request of the player.

8. If a player plays one stroke with the wrong ball, he shall go back and play again without penalty; if more than one stroke, he shall in match play lose the hole; in stroke play lose two strokes and finish the hole with the wrong ball. If two players in match play each play the wrong ball, they shall finish the hole thus and the scores shall stand.

9. The club may be grounded anywhere except in a sand bunker.

10. No penalty shall be incurred for, by mistake, (1) hitting a moving ball, (2) playing from in front of the teebox, (3) touching the sand in a bunker, (4) playing out of turn, (5) moving the ball. In the case of (5) the ball shall be replaced, the player ensuring, as always, that no advantage to himself accrues.

'Distinguished Stranger'

Chance has just favoured me with an experience which every golfer, I am sure, will envy—namely, an hour in his home with J. H. Taylor. He lives on the hill in Northam, looking down upon what he declares to be 'the finest view in Christendom'—the links of Westward Ho! where he began as a caddie boy eighty years ago, with the broad expanse of the Atlantic in the background.

His room reflects the story of his life. The eye of the visitor is caught by an illuminated scroll from the Hants and Isle of Wight Golfing Association commending his splendid play in winning his second successive Open Championship in 1895—he was professional at Winchester at the time—and, next to it, a picture of him and Harry Vardon at the front door of Muirfield, taken the following year just before Vardon beat him on a play off and prevented his doing the hat-trick.

Another illuminated scroll arrived sixty years later—and what a charming gesture it was!—from all the competitors in the United States Professional Seniors' Championship. There must be upwards of 200 signatures on it. Then there is J. H. with W. G. Grace—perhaps the two most celebrated sporting figures to be known in their own sphere inevitably by their initials. This picture, taken at Royal Mid-Surrey early in J. H.'s forty-six years' association with the club, reveals the familiar bearded figure wearing plus-fours and his ringed cricket cap. J. H. believes it to be the only one in existence showing the master cricketer holding a golf club and he has bequeathed it to the M.C.C.

Yet of all his trophies I dare say the one of which he is most proud is the framed letter from the Royal and Ancient Club of St. Andrews inviting him to be an honorary member. It quotes the rule of the club which empowers the committee to extend such an invitation to 'Princes of the Blood Royal and other distinguished strangers'.

As befits one who was reared in the shadow of the United Services College, which was the background of *Stalky and Co.*, J. H. is a devoted admirer of Kipling. Those who were brought up on Stalky, McTurk and Beetle will remember the luckless master, Mr. Prout. His real name was Pugh and as a little boy J. H. used to wear his cast-off trousers, suitably adapted by his mother.

He has a letter from Kipling, in which he says 'those were good old days when the Burrows were free to all and, as you remember, we golfed when and where we chose and there were very few books or theories to confuse the mind or the muscles'. The black and white Taylor cat, I noted, is called Rikki, after Rikki Tikki Tavi.

To the traditionalist it is a thrill as well as a privilege to listen to J. H. His mind is clear as a bell and he recalls with amazing clarity and no trace of romanticism incidents in his golfing life which took place before men who are sixty now were born. He was, for instance, the first English professional ever to hit a rubber-cored ball.

He and Vardon were at the Wheaton Club, Chicago, in 1900 and Mr. Haskell sent him some samples of the balls which were to bear that name—and incidentally to split the golfing world in two.

J. H. drove one in the direction of a green 220 yards away, on which some people were putting. He drove straight in among them and had to go running, cap in hand, to apologize. It was an unprecedented hit. Vardon won the U.S. Championship. 'I was too timid, sir. I was too timid,' said

J. H., thumping the arm of his chair. 'Without a shadow of
a doubt I should have beaten Vardon if I had played with
that ball.'

They came home for the British Open at Hoylake and still
he did not play with it. Soon the new-fangled balls were
fetching as much as 30s. apiece—a fantastic sum in those days.
Sandy Herd borrowed one from John Ball. Its rubber entrails were hanging out all over the place and it was the only
one he had. He played all four rounds with it—and won.

Standing beside the fireplace is the driving-iron with
which J.H. played one of the most written-about shots in
golf—his second to the sixth hole, or Briars, at Hoylake in
1913. With a tremendous wind blowing, he carried the
garden and nearly knocked the flag out of the hole. 'The
ball,' wrote A. C. Croome at the time, 'seemed to make a
hole in the wind as it bored its way along.' The club still has
its original hickory shaft but it now bears a brass inscription.
J.H. gave it to be auctioned for St. Mary's Hospital, Pad-
dington. Sold and resold, it fetched more than £100, and
the last buyers gave it back to him as a memento.

'How much did it cost?' I asked him. 'Five and sixpence,'
he replied. 'We could make you the best irons in the world
for five and six. Sometimes,' he added with a twinkle, 'we
stamped "special" on them. Then they were seven and six.'
As to the cost of clubs today—more thumping on the arm-
chair and 'Iniquitous, sir. Iniquitous!'

There was so much more that I wish I had space to tell.
Suffice to say that what really warmed my heart—to say
nothing of J.H.'s—was the huge pile of telegrams arising
from my recent mention of his eighty-eighth birthday. When
I left, I felt I was indeed saying good-bye to the Grand Old
Man of Golf.

Beating your Age

Starting as a boy under that great green-keeper, Tom Bridges, before the latter went to Hoylake, Jim Morris has been at Huntercombe for well over fifty years. They have a tournament named after him, in which the lady members have first to beat him in a match in order to qualify to play each other in a knock-out competition. Morris plays from scratch, gives them their full handicap and starts them two up.

We hear much about people 'going round in their age' but few do it in competitive play with every putt holed out. James Braid was always doing it at Walton Heath, but perhaps the most noted instance was Sandy Herd holing Moor Park in 67 in a professional tournament on the eve of his seventieth birthday; an achievement which I remember wringing from a young professional the bitter comment: 'I'm about a quarter his —— age and I —— well take 79.'

Jim Morris will be sixty-nine next month. Last week he was duly challenged by Mrs. E. M. Wood, who received her full 31 shots and two up. He beat her by 4 and 3 and, all holed out, went round in 66.

The Huntercombe bogey is 72 and the scratch score 70, and I can assure you that if you can play to your handicap there you can play to it anywhere. Morris's score was:

434334444–33
444443343–33–66

For sustained accuracy this was a remarkable round, since he took 29 putts. This means that he had 37 other shots. With three short holes and one long one out of range in two shots, the absolute minimum by which he could reach every green was 33. He therefore missed the green with approach shots of any distance only four times, two of these being at short holes, where he took 4. Has anyone in golfing history, I wonder, ever done a round in which he hit every green in the right number? It would be interesting to know. And has anyone else done a genuine 66 at the age of sixty-eight and eleven months?

My first thought on looking at Morris's card was 'I wonder if he has improved his eclectic score?' As it turned out he had not—but it would have been almost a miracle if he had. As a kind of celestial vision of golf, here is the hole-by-hole score which he has accumulated over a lifetime at Huntercombe:

$$313231233-21$$
$$331332332-23-44$$

Is this unique? Can any veteran, professional or amateur, match it anywhere? If not what is the nearest? We should all like to know.

*

Having quoted last week the eclectic score of 44 by Jim Morris, the professional at Huntercombe, I ventured to ask whether anyone could improve on it. Frankly I doubted it— but how little I knew. Why, 44, it seems, is positively commonplace. Even amateurs can beat it, though many, having taken a lifetime to do so, add wryly, 'I can hardly hope to improve on it now.'

More than one correspondent has been good enough to send me that excellent booklet entitled *How to Play the Old Course at St. Andrews*, which quotes Andra Kirkaldy's score of 43, compiled over fifty years of play with a gutty. Whether the figures are authentic or as apocryphal as I always suspect so many of the stories of that rugged character to be, I cannot say, but since so many people all over the world know the Old Course I venture to quote them in full:

232332312–21
212342332–22

A member of Sidmouth, which I believe to be somewhat on the short side, though doubtless most congenial, tells me that their professional, Cyril Easterbrook, who is 'much too modest to tell you himself', has an eclectic of 34—this fantastic score being made up of 3 ones, 14 twos and 1 three. Gullane No. 1 is a more formidable proposition and more than one person has told me of the remarkable achievement of Willie Gilchrist thereon. Mr. Gilchrist, who was the proprietor of two hotels there, has played approximately 10,000 rounds at Gullane, as a result of which he comes out with an eclectic of 36—out in 19, home in 17: 3 ones, 3 threes and the rest twos. He has twice done the seventeenth (393 yards) in two—'one a bit lucky, the other a good one.'

Two notable scores come from the Olton Club, Warwickshire, whose course used to measure 6,040 yards but is now, I gather, rather longer, with a scratch score of 72. Hugh Boyle, when assistant there—he is now assistant at the Berkshire Club—contrived a score of 45 in the space of a mere three years, beginning when he was only nineteen. The other is in many ways the most extraordinary of the lot. It comes from Mr. John Horden.

Some friends in the club before the war were talking of eclectic scores and with them he began to work out his own. He discovered that he had done every hole in two and that his total was therefore 36. Eighteen twos *must* surely be a record!

He also discovered that every two except one had been done in a competition and, furthermore, in the presence of a member of the present company. They procured a scorecard and, signing their names as witness against the appropriate holes, presented it to him as a souvenir.

Apologizing for his vile typing (which I thought was rather good for an amateur), Mr. Horden adds a comment which I am sure will strike a chord with every golfer who has tried to play with the malady at present afflicting my correspondent. 'I have an acute stiff neck,' he writes, 'and I find that it creates the same kind of problem in typing as in golf: that is to say, if I position myself so that I can see what I am aiming at, I can't hit it; if I position myself so that I *can* hit it, then I can't see it!'

Apart from Mr. Gilchrist's homeward half of 17 at Gullane, some of the 9-hole scores are really astonishing. Mr. W. C. Simpson, has 19 for the first nine (3,010 yards) at Royal Mid-Surrey, slipping back to a modest 25 for the second—he also quotes L. H. Taylor, son of 'J.H.' as having a total of 43. I wonder what J.H.'s own eclectic was in his forty-odd years at Mid-Surrey?

Dr. T. D. Burt, president of the Reddish Vale Club, is quoted by a member as having 17 for the first nine (2,795 yards) but all in a way are capped by Mr. J. W. Nelson, of the North Hants Club at Fleet who, seventy-five next month, is among those who 'can hardly hope to improve on it now'. His total is 40—home in 18—but here, just for the 'pleasure of seeing them on paper, are his figures for the nine consecutive holes from the eighth to the sixteenth, which include three short holes and three others of 454, 434 and 428 yards:

121222212–15

Nor can I resist quoting the effort of a former green-keeper-cum-professional of a nine-hole course in Kirkcudbrightshire which, says a correspondent from Edinburgh, 'is about 2,800 yards and must be among the worst in the United Kingdom, but with wonderful views. . . .' This stalwart did six ones and three twos—total 12.

One cannot help being struck by the number of really long shots that must be holed at golf which one never hears about, simply because they were not done at a short hole, from a tee, and are therefore not holes in one. Mr. Horden, for instance, must have holed shots of every description among his 18 twos at Olton—but never had a 'one'.

The distribution of 'ones' seems quite unaccountable. Sandy Herd did 19, James Braid 18, and J. H. Taylor 10. Yet Harry Vardon, indisputably the greatest player of his age, did only one; Walter Hagen, incredibly, did only one and Walter Travis, three times Amateur Champion of the U.S. and once of Great Britain, never did one at all.

If golf survives long enough with millions of people playing incessantly all over the world, one has visions, rather on the lines of the chimpanzee eventually typing the complete works of Shakespeare, of everything happening at last to the same man on the same day—the first authentic score to break 40. Then we can all pack up.

OOS-M

Here we go Again!

'B.O.A.C. announce the departure of their Britannia service to New York, Flight 581.' In a few hours I hope to be hearing the familiar call and if it ever ceases to thrill I shall know that the time has come to call it a day. It is indeed an agreeable prospect—the thought of the Californian desert and another Ryder Cup match, hard beside where the last one was played in America four years ago. This time the scene is to be the Eldorado Club.

What extraordinary people the Americans are! Only six weeks ago a friend was writing from Eldorado to say that, while the course had weathered the severest part of the summer, the club-house, which is to be 'very large, very unusual and very expensive', was not even finished! This is well in keeping with the carefree spirit which comes over the most serious of people after a few days in the desert and is only one of the reasons for its rapidly becoming the playground of Western America.

It is not, in fact, desert at all but the most extraordinarily fertile ground, once you can find water. This they discovered 500 ft. underground a few years ago and since then golf courses, complete with full-size imported palm trees, have been springing up all over the place. I will quote for positively the last time the remark of the man whom I saw four years ago watering the two-inch high grass in front of his house, which he declared he had planted only a fortnight before.

'Yes, sir,' he said, 'in these parts all you have to do is sow the seed, apply the water—and jump back.'

Palm Springs, California

Since we were here four years ago, no fewer than eleven courses have sprung up in the desert. Of these, Eldorado is by far the most notable as well as the most ambitious. Architects of the course and part owners of the club are Jimmy Hines, lately professional at Thunderbird where the last match was played, and Johnny Dawson, Walker Cup player and semifinalist in our championship at Sandwich thirty years ago.

Scenically, they have done a wonderful job, deliberately aligning many of the holes to face through an avenue of palms directly towards one of the snow-capped 10,000 foot peaks in the distance.

Two years ago the site was a citrus ranch. European architects will gnash their teeth on hearing that only six months and one week later the course was in such perfect condition that it was possible to take a driver from the fairway. Every possible grapefruit tree has been left intact and the fruit looks extremely tempting but unfortunately is still green.

The course is a full 7,000 yards and is going to prove a real teaser, since many of the greens have been flanked by water instead of sand. This was a bold decision, which I can foresee causing a good deal of wailing. The modern professional, spoilt by the wedge, can splash the ball out of loose sand time and again within a few feet of the hole. You cannot splash it dead out of three feet of water.

Each year as the Bermuda grass browns off they sow the whole course with a finer variety of rye and this year for the first time carried out the operation by air. One aviator, nipping off the tops of two palm trees in the process, did it all in two days, and the grass was being mown ten days later. The only trouble was that the seed also settled on the water hazards and grew a lawn on top of them as well.

Unbeknown to each other, the American captain, Sam Snead, and I arrived in the same aeroplane together a couple of days ahead of the rest. Next day he made his expenses against three club members by 'shooting' 68, a score which I cannot see often being beaten in the match itself. He knows the course, since it was here that he recently played and was beaten by Gary Player in the 'all star' series which is one of the most popular programmes on American television.

Few clubs can have been so thoroughly put on the map in the second year of their existence, not only by this programme and the Ryder Cup but also by a recent six-day visit by President Eisenhower, who stayed with a friend nearby and played every day. There seems no doubt that he arrived looking rather frail and left as fit as a fiddle. His best nine holes were 39 and 41, though not in the same round.

The last-minute work on the club-house could hardly be imagined by one who did not see it. Even on Thursday 150 men were still at work hammering at the roof, creating flower beds and unwrapping the furniture from its covers. It is, of course, luxurious beyond anything conceivable in our own climate, but all is in impeccable taste.

At some aspects of golf as played in these parts we may perhaps be permitted a faint, though I trust not patronizing smile. Any idea of actually walking round the course is, of course, unthinkable. The electric buggies are housed in a special underground garage and when a member wishes to play, his cart and clubs are brought briskly up the ramp to the 1st tee. A closed circuit TV, believe it or not, enables the starter to see the 1st and 10th tees and send forth the players accordingly.

To my great regret these carts are to be banned during the matches, and I shall have either to walk or sit on the terrace, from which, I am assured, at least 1,000 people can see four of the greens.

I am living, only temporarily alas, in one of the cottages fringing the course amid their own trees, lawns and flowers. These are quite exquisite and anyone can have one for the equivalent of £14,000. The maid in trim white overalls has just, as I write, scooted up on her electric cart, complete with portable vacuum cleaner, to do my room.

I had hoped to conclude with some description of the British team's early form and reaction to the course, but after their really terrifying experience in the air between Los Angeles and here overnight, they emerged pale and wan in the morning and most spent the day recuperating.

'I must have flown nearly a million miles,' said Dai Rees, 'and I have never seen anything like it.'

Caught in a thunderstorm, the tail end of the hurricane which has been devastating Mexico, their plane was tossed about to such an extent that their baggage hit the roof and the stewardess was quickly rendered insensible. They endured more than an hour of this before the plane turned back, and it is clear that another sporting disaster on Manchester United lines was only narrowly averted.

Considering their previous buffeting in the *Queen Elizabeth* and eight days of continuous travel, speech making and receptions, there is no doubt that the team's immediate pre-occupations must be rest and physical fitness rather than golf. Through no fault of their own they have indeed got off to a shaky start.[1]

Honolulu

Golf certainly has become a world-wide game. This morning I have been up to the Oahu Country Club, the oldest golf club west of Chicago, to see the opening stages of the Hawaiian Open Championship, and at least 75 per cent of the 90 entrants were Orientals.

The Japanese, fired perhaps by their natural success in the Canada Cup two years ago, seem to have gone mad on the game. The driving range in the park here is crowded all day and people queue for a starting time on the public course well before daylight.

The club-house, incidentally, is named after my host,

[1] Britain were beaten by 7 matches to 2, with three halved.

Francis Brown, a familiar figure each year at Gleneagles, where he is generally known as 'Pineapple'. He was once amateur champion simultaneously of California, Hawaii and Japan and, at the age of sixty-one, holed the first nine at Pebble Beach in 29. This shook him so severely that he took four putts on the tenth green and came home in 41.

I cast my mind back to the Ryder Cup with mixed feelings. Without seeking to blame anyone in particular, one can see that the team's preparation for the match included elementary mistakes which will be easily avoidable in future.

The Eldorado course, on which I played a number of rounds, slopes almost imperceptibly from the mountain end to the desert end and the greens are incredibly difficult to read—indeed I do not remember a course on which I have found it so difficult to judge the line to the hole. The longest possible period of practice, therefore, was essential.

Instead, the team spent five days at sea, took a bus to Atlantic City and played with local amateurs in a rainstorm. They then flew to Washington, played two more courses with amateurs and then did the same in Atlanta before flying across the continent to Los Angeles. They received all along the line the heart-warming hospitality one expects in America and if they were killed by kindness before they got started they have only their own management to blame.

In the end they had only six days in which to settle down and learn the course, and three of these were taken up with pro-amateur competitions. In the match itself I saw putt after putt hit perfectly well yet miss the hole through being on the wrong line. I do not say that with a longer preparation the British team would have won; of course, they wouldn't, but I do think they would have made a stronger impression. At any rate I hope that when the Walker Cup team go to Seattle in 1961 they will fly straight over the Pole and have done with it.

Dai Rees, who made an admirable captain, would I think agree with these views, since his own fine recovery from six down only ended in failure through his putt for a 3 on the thirty-sixth green being hit on the wrong line. Of the rest of the team, apart from that redoubtable fighter Eric Brown, who added a fourth successive scalp to his bag in the singles, thus setting a record unsurpassed on either side, I should single out for special credit Norman Drew, Peter Alliss and David Thomas, each of whom came out with added stature.

Perth, W. Australia

The first 10,000 miles of my homeward journey leave memories of Viscounts—surely one of the great aircraft of all time—singing like kettles all over New Zealand and Australia and proceeding with the regularity of suburban trains, and periods on the ground being subjected to the most warm-hearted hospitality of friends old and new.

Much of this, naturally enough, has occurred at golf clubs, the farthest afield being the Shirley Club at Christchurch, where, I am happy to report, the Governor-General and I, through His Excellency holing a dubious five footer on the last green, came out victorious.

Lord Cobham, whose two shots to the seventh green in the University match of 1932 are still spoken of with awe at Royal Lytham, remains the longest hitter with whom I have personally played. He could not perhaps have outhit the vast American, George Bayer, who I imagine hit the ball farther than anyone in the game's history, but in a memorable single at Mildenhall he did consistently outdrive Arthur Lacey in his prime.

His appointment as Governor-General seemed at the time to be an inspired one, and so it turned out. I can truthfully say that in all my travels I have heard no man spoken of with such unanimous affection and respect.

It is a commonplace that most New Zealanders look upon England—or, in the case of Dunedin, Scotland—as 'home'. The reverse is also true in that the traveller round the world from England finds himself never so close to home as when he is in fact farthest from it.

The feeling was intensified by a visit to the Heretaunga Club outside Wellington, where I found that the secretary

Mr. Bob Raylor, had come from the Newcastle Club, County Down, and the professional, John Watt, an ex-fighter pilot, from Aberdeen. With the mountain background and a river full of trout dashing alongside, this idyllic spot, which might have been a remote Highland valley in midsummer, provided a remarkable and welcome contrast to the hurly-burly of the original objects of the present expedition, the tournaments for the Ryder and Canada Cups.

Turning for home, I enjoyed a brief interlude in Adelaide, where they showed me a new pitch and putt course almost in the heart of the city, and now, after flying over hundreds upon hundreds of miles of nothing at all, have reached what one has always been told to be the fairest city in Australia. First impressions, certainly, confirm this view.

The Royal Perth Club is hard beside the Swan River and the breeze blowing in across the estuary dispels not only the heat of the mid-day sun but also the most persistent flies in the world, for which the city, alas, is notorious. For really first-class golf enclosed in a confined space without giving one a feeling of being cramped, one could search the world without finding a course better than Perth.

My partner here was Miss Maxine Bishop, champion of both Australia and New Zealand in 1951, whom many will remember at home and who is now a 'comptometerist' manipulating complicated figures on a machine in the British Petroleum Company here. Her eminence caused the appearance of a television cameraman and may have revealed to me yet again the secret of golf. He was short of film, he said, so my drive consisted of one brief address and a carefree swing with an exhibition follow through. The ball sped as though fired from a rifle, the best drive for several years. It seemed an awful long way to have to come to find out.

Johannesburg

Although I seem to remember Mr. John Beck having played an evening round at Winged Foot outside New York and another next morning at the Berkshire, it may also be unusual, to say the least of it, to play within the space of three days at Perth (Australia) and Johannesburg. The intervening twenty-four hours were occupied in traversing the 6,435 miles of ocean by which they are separated.

This involved stops at Cocos Island, of which at midnight one sees little worthy of recall except a few palm trees and a notice over the door saying 'Altitude ten feet', and then 2,877 miles further on—which I believe to be the longest scheduled oversea flight in the world—the lovely island of Mauritius, which, to the surprise of at least one uneducated traveller, the French, who seem to own most of it, call 'Maurice'.

At Karrinyup, only a few miles from the centre of Perth, I found what was far and away the most attractive course which I have seen in Australasia. It rather resembles Wentworth. In the centre is a lake, complete with many varieties of wild fowl, including the black swan, which forms the official crest both of the city and its renowned brewery.

In the spring, namely September, the rough is covered with a vast carpet of wild flowers and my partner told me that he had picked eight different kinds of orchid in the course of a single round.

The Royal Johannesburg Club, which was accorded its prefix after a visit by the then Prince of Wales in 1925, is set in a softer setting with a background of Lombardy poplars, weeping willows and hydrangeas, and possesses the only 'fine' grass I have seen outside the British Isles. This will not grow in any part of the United States or the Antipodes, so we probably do not appreciate how lucky we are.

The club was founded seventy years ago when, incredibly to anyone sitting in the heart of the modern city, Johannesburg consisted of a few rough huts erected beside the new gold-mines. One cannot help assuming that among those in search of the gold were a number of Scotsmen, for one of the first things they did was to lay out a golf course, sinking empty condensed milk tins in what they were pleased to call the greens.

As the city grew they were pushed farther and farther out

—an all too familiar tale all over the world today—on one occasion removing their club-house bodily by ox-wagon. From these humble beginnings there sprang what is now the senior club in the Union.

Royal Johannesburg was the scene a month ago of the second Commonwealth Tournament, the first having been inaugurated in 1954 to celebrate the 200th birthday of the Royal and Ancient Club of St. Andrews. This event clashed precisely with the Ryder Cup match, to which, since we were the holders of the trophy, I felt it my duty to go. I wa⁻ particularly pleased, therefore, to have a chance of coming here so soon after the tournament when it was fresh in so many people's minds.

Two or three years after the first Commonwealth Tournament, the Eisenhower Trophy was inaugurated. As this included nations from all over the world, and as money, time and players are not in inexhaustible supply, it was widely felt that the Commonwealth event probably, though of course regrettably, would have to go by the board. Only an outstanding success in 1959, together with a unanimous and enthusiastic desire to continue could save it.

Both the Eisenhower Trophy and its professional counterpart, the Canada Cup, have two unavoidable defects. One, which does not matter much, is that the players are of such widely differing ability; the other, which does, is that they do not all speak a common language. With the best will in the world, you cannot exude goodwill to a fellow who cannot understand a word you say—or a word for that matter of the complimentary speeches that are poured forth at the dinner.

The Commonwealth Tournament has neither of these defects. The golf is a hard-fought battle between near equals and everyone has not only a common language but a common heritage. From every source, including the Australian manager, Justin Seward, whom I met on his return home, I gain the impression that the tournament here was such a success as to engender a universal determination that it shall go on whatever may be the cost and whatever else may have to be sacrificed. To me, since I have always looked on it as one of the most worthwhile events in golf, this is good news indeed.

Not such good news is that which we have been receiving from home, to which I am destined all too soon to be whisked in a matter of hours by one of B.O.A.C.'s newly inaugurated Comets.[1] Blizzard, gale and fog appear to be the order of the day and to one who yesterday saw the first shower of rain for nearly two months this is an ominous prospect. Oh to be out of England now that December's there.

[1] It was due in London at 1.35 p.m. The wheels touched down at 1.32 and the motors were switched off at 1.37.

In the Drink

Speaking at a dinner the other evening, Mr. P. B. Lucas, D.S.O., D.F.C., recalled that he had previously been invited to speak at the dinner of the same society's swimming club and proceeded to analyse the surprisingly close association between golf—if not golfers—and water. It proved to be a fruitful theme, with which in a golfing career that began at the age of five he could claim a fairly varied connection.

He mentioned Pine Valley, which he visited with the 1936 Walker Cup team, though without in fact playing in the match. This is a great 'water' course, with one short hole a complete island except for a single narrow footpath and another with a vast carry over a lake.

Here he was so often in woods or water that an American paper entitled him the 'Southpaw sprayer'. I should add perhaps in fairness that another speaker at the dinner referred to him, and I think rightly, as 'the only left-hander who ever looked like a golfer'.[1]

In a pro-amateur tournament in Florida, he went on, his professional partner sliced into a creek at the eighteenth and found his ball in a flat-bottomed boat, which he solemnly

[1] This, I need hardly say, was before New Zealander Bob Charles won the 1963 Open Championship.

176

punted to a position level with the green, chipped out of, and holed the putt for a four.

Perhaps his most engaging reminiscence was of the occasion when he was 'knocked off' by a cannon shell at 30,000 feet while returning from escorting an American raid on Lille. As he was contemplating jumping out of his Spitfire, losing stroke and distance, the white cliffs of Ramsgate hove in view, reminding him that he knew every inch of the course at Prince's, Sandwich—indeed he was born in the club-house—and could perhaps put the machine down on the first fairway.

He overshot this, and then the old sixth, and then the ninth—farthest point of the course—and eventually came to rest in a ditch in the marsh—out of bounds yet again!

Water engenders more violent emotions in the golfer's heart than any other hazard. The futility of hitting it into the pond, followed by the slow humiliation of having to fish it out with a wire contraption on the end of a pole, or worse still being able to see it but not reach it, certain in the knowledge that some enterprising small boy will have gone in and got it by the morning, gives one what the Americans call the 'slow burn' to a degree unmatched by the fiercest heather or gorse.

Many occasions come to mind. I did not see the Oxford player who flung his clubs into the lake at Stoke Poges, but I did see a Cambridge undergraduate knee-deep in the stream beside the fifth at Mildenhall, trying to retrieve his putter in order to continue playing in the Trials—and, furthermore, I once met a fellow who claimed to be the original of the story of the man who, after an unsuccessful foray in Scotland, flung his clubs into the Firth of Forth one by one from the carriage window, followed by the bag.

The Swilcan Burn at St. Andrews has been the scene, of course, of innumerable tragi-comedies of golf, none better than that of the man who, playing it as the nineteenth, fluffed into it three times. He threw his clubs in, so it is said; then he threw his caddie in; then jumped in himself. The only man really to get the better of the Burn, as I like to think, was a celebrated Australian professional. He dismissed it with the comment that he had 'got in the drink at the first'.

One water hazard which took its place in history almost before it was built is the artificial kidney-shaped pond, already stocked with fish, into which poor Harry Weetman hit his second shot at the last hole during the Ryder Cup match at Eldorado. This was one of seven or eight similar hazards guarding the four greens that border on the clubhouse and one of the reasons for installing them, instead of sand, was to prevent players from 'skimming' shots by mistake into the assembled company on the terrace.

Many of the professionals, especially the Americans who are so adept at splashing out of sand bunkers, gnashed their teeth at the very sight of them and declared them to be unfair, but to me they were the greatest of fun and I should like to see golf enlivened by more of them. But then I wasn't playing in the match.

Centenary Open

In a fantastically exciting finish Kel Nagle, of Australia, won the Centenary Open Golf Championship of 1960 on the Old course at St. Andrews with a final round of 71 and a total of 278 for the 72 holes, beating by one stroke Arnold Palmer, the American champion, who had a magnificent last round of 68.

What a thrilling, wonderful and wholly unforgettable championship! It was as though fate had intervened to flood the course yesterday in order to build up a finish that will live forever in the memory of all who saw it.

Challengers threatened for a moment and faded from the picture till in the end, nine holes from home, it was clearly a three-cornered battle between Palmer, and, playing together just behind him, de Vicenzo, of the Argentine, and Nagle. When they started, it was Nagle 207, Vicenzo 209, Palmer 211.

Palmer, the most hardened competitor of the three and perhaps the world's leading golfer of the day, was probably better equipped to spend an unforeseeable extra night sleeping on the prospect of the final round. Whatever he did, the other two, since he would be playing ahead of them, would know about it within seconds.

He started as he meant to go on, with a pitch to the first hole almost stone dead, and the distant cheers were echoing in the ears of Vicenzo and Nagle as they drove off. Each took 4 and there was one stroke of their precious lead gone.

Frankly, I suspected that both might crack under the strain. In the event, Vicenzo could not quite stand it but Nagle acquitted himself like a man. He never wavered.

Briefly, all three were out in 34, a highly respectable score in the circumstances, which in fact was only twice bettered. Still level. When Vicenzo failed to get his 3 at the eleventh, the second of the only two short holes, it was clear that he was beginning to trail and now it was a straight fight.

Palmer struck a horrid blow with a 3 at the thirteenth, reducing Nagle's lead to three, and at the long fourteenth which, from the back tee, has taken the place of the seventeenth as the fateful hole on the Old course, Nagle, as he was the first to admit, was definitely lucky.

His drive lay above ground in the midst of the deep bunkers known as the 'Beardies' and he was able to get his 5. He took three putts on the fifteenth, and now the lead was down to 2.

Palmer holed the seventeenth in 4 and hit the biggest drive of the day at the eighteenth. I felt absolutely certain that this fine young man, who is probably mentally the toughest competitor in golf today, would get a three. He pitched up within six feet and his putt, across a right-hand slope, went slam bang into the middle of the hole.

As the cheers—and very sincere ones at that—echoed round the buildings round the last green with every window, roof and chimney-pot manned, we could see Nagle facing a seven-footer for his 4 on the seventeenth. A 5 here and he would be left with 4 to tie. If ever a putt won a championship this one did—again right in the middle.

He hit a good drive to the eighteenth and the spectators, claiming their traditional privilege, swarmed across the fairway. In dead silence he pitched up with a 9-iron—within three feet! Another stampede and there he was, a lone figure in his moment of triumph. Two to win the Centenary Open from three feet. Well, he needed both, but never mind. It was a wonderful performance, rendered all the better by his warm tributes later to his less fortunate fellow-countryman, four times winner, Peter Thomson.

The winner is a fine, unassuming golfer, and a delightful ambassador for his country. As to the runner-up, I have never known a great American player who made such a universally favourable impression on his first visit and I only hope he will keep his promise to come and see us again soon.

*

No one who saw the Open Championship, either in person, or I dare say, on the television, is likely ever to forget it. As the years go on and senility approaches, I find that I forget, of postwar championships, whether it was a 'Thomson Year' or a 'Locke Year', but I shall remember the Centenary Open to my dying day as the 'Nagle-nearly-Palmer-Year'.

I should like to pay a personal tribute to each. Within a few minutes of his triumph I recorded a seven or eight-minute talk with Nagle for transmission on Australian television. He held the trophy in one hand and the special Centenary replica—a most beautiful work of art—in the other, and it was *his* championship. Yet he spent most of the time paying tribute to Peter Thomson—all the help he had given him over the years, how he had piloted him round the Old course, and how he had won four championships against his, Nagle's, one. One's heart warmed towards him.

Of Palmer one can only say that he must be not only the world's leading golfer, with untold successes ahead, but also one of the most approachable and unassuming of men. He said just the right things about the Old course (whatever he may have thought!) and did not even revolt when a newspaper asked if they could take a photograph of him in bed. Everyone hoped that we should see him and his charming wife again.[1]

[1] We did. He won the next two open championships, at Birkdale and Troon, and continued to say 'exactly the right things'.

Peter Thomson Tells all

I say without hesitation that this is just about the best, and certainly the most succinct, piece of golfing instruction that I have ever read. There is no lack of modesty in this assertion, since, as you will see, Thomson's contribution is everything and the writer's virtually nothing. My own part in the proceedings was to spend a couple of half-hours with him in the lounge of Rusack's Hotel at St. Andrews and then set down what he said almost precisely as he said it. As seen, described, and played by Thomson, golf is indeed a simple game. It is the rest of us who make it so difficult!

All this began in a practice round before the recent Bowmaker tournament at Sunningdale. Though I had watched him many dozens of times, this was the first time that I had had the pleasure actually of playing with Peter Thomson. I had always found it difficult to describe his style to other people because it seemed so straightforward. There was nothing peculiar about it. It turned out not only that his ideas about the golf swing were as 'simple' as his method but also, as I hope to prove, that he was equally good at communicating them.

I asked him, naturally, to cast an eye over my own manifestly unsatisfactory efforts and he said at once, 'Well, for a start you are set up all wrong.'

This expression, 'getting set up right', constitutes the

absolute basis of Thomson's golf. 'If you get set up right and look like a competent golfer, you won't go nearly so far wrong.' Your set-up consists of how you stand, where you are aiming, your 'triangle' (i.e. the two arms and shoulders), and where you put the ball in relation to your feet.

The nearer you are, before you start, to the position in which you will be when you hit the ball, the fewer adjustments you will have to make in the course of the shot. 'Think how your body has to be when you strike the ball,' he says, 'and work back from there.' Lest this sounds too obvious, take a look on the 1st tee on a Sunday morning and see how many people's starting position bears any relation to any position in which they could conceivably be at impact!

There is no reason why any of us, tall or short, fat or thin, should not get set up right. The stance, about which volumes have been written, is a piece of typical Thomsonian simplicity. Lay a club down on the ground, pointing to the hole, and put your toes against it. That is the end of that.

Now put the ball opposite your left foot with your left arm and the club in a straight line, as they will be, or should be, as you actually hit the ball. Your arm and the club will now be at right-angles to the imaginary club on the ground against which you have lined up your toes. If they are not, you have got the ball—*as almost everyone has*—too far back. (We are talking at the moment of wooden club shots.)

We now come to the critical point, the make-or-mar of the entire set-up. Your right arm is not long enough. It won't reach. How are you going to get it on to the club?

You do it instinctively as nature tells you, the easiest way. You reach *over* with the right hand, bringing the right shoulder forward in the process, and at the same time, probably without realizing it, you bring the left hand back a bit to meet it. This is perfectly comfortable, but, to make it more so, you probably move forward a couple of inches at the last moment, thus, in effect, bringing the ball two inches back.

The whole set-up is now wrecked.

Let us retrace our steps. The right arm once again is not

long enough. This time, keeping your right shoulder back and tilting your left shoulder up, you reach *under* with the right hand and attach it to the club. (This was accompanied in the *Sunday Times* by a picture of myself, taken on my lawn and bearing the caption, 'I don't care what you say—I at least *look* like a golfer'.)

I tried this experiment on many willing subjects and in every case, regardless of handicap, in this position they at once looked like a golfer. If it feels awkward at first, it only shows how wrong you were before. You can apply a simple test. When you have got 'set up', keep your body still, lay the club flat across your chest and see where it is pointing. In the 'easy' position you will find that it points yards to the left of the hole. If you are set up right, it will be pointing straight at the flag.

HOW FAR AWAY FROM THE BALL SHOULD YOU BE?

Thomson often uses the expression 'measuring off'. You will notice that he himself measures off quite deliberately before each shot. Stand relaxed, leaning slightly forward, with your knees slightly bent and the whole body *in balance*. Extend the left arm and the club in a straight line, not stiff as a ramrod, and you are now measured off. 'Picture in mind your position as you strike the ball and make final adjustments from that.' This applies to every club.

HOW DO YOU GRIP THE CLUB?

Again, delightfully simple. *Get set up right and you won't notice!* Take it as you find it.

HOW HARD DO YOU HOLD ON TO THE CLUB?

'Often,' says Thomson, 'you can actually *see* the tension in a man's hand. You should start with a light touch, barely enough to lift it off the ground—so that it feels heavy. It is just like using an axe. You lift it with a light grip, just enough to raise it, and it feels heavy. As you bring it down, your grip tightens without your thinking about it and reaches its tightest at the moment of impact.

184

'There is another likeness with golf. Using an axe, you do not *hit* with it; you *accelerate* it. That is exactly what you should do with a golf club.'

HOW DO YOU START THE CLUB BACK?

'Well, you just *draw it straight back*. Never mind about what the books din into you about turns and pivots. Just draw it straight back as far as is comfortable and let nature take its course. Don't turn away; just draw it back—*but*—keep your weight squarely on both feet and make sure you don't sway back with it yourself.'

Finally, what Thomson describes as the key axiom in the golf swing, namely, to be behind the ball when you strike it—not all of you, maybe, but certainly your head. '*A plumb line from your nose as you strike the ball should hit the ground several inches behind it*'—a sobering thought for us lurchers and swayers, to whom, as we heave forward, the ball so often appears to be moving rapidly backwards.

As a postscript I might add that, with the first shot in which Thomson was satisfied that he had got me satisfactorily 'set-up', I ricked my back—probably using muscles which had not come into play for thirty years—to such an extent that we almost had to terminate the game there and then. This in no way shook my faith in his principles and I wish you the best of luck. You have been warned![1]

*

I described last week the emphasis placed by Peter Thomson —to whom congratulations on winning in the meanwhile the

[1] A few days after publication of the above, in July, I had a letter from a reader in Yorkshire. He had tried it on the lawn on a wet day, he said, and, having only slippers on, had fallen flat on his face. He had retired to the house, changed into spiked shoes, and tried again. 'I then had to be helped back into the house. The doctor was summoned and he says that, given reasonable care, I should be able to play again in October.'

German Open Championship—on how important it is to get 'set up' right before making a golf shot. The example taken was a wooden club shot, but the same principle applies to all.

We are to imagine the position in which we shall be, or ought to be, when we hit the ball, and set ourselves up as nearly in that position as possible. It will involve, as always, the left arm and the club in a straight line, rather as though one were about to play a one-armed shot with the left arm.

The position of the ball with the driver was simple. It was opposite the left foot. Where is it to be with the other clubs? Again there are no complications. His answer is '*roughly an inch farther back for each club*'.

This finds the ball mid-way between the feet with a 5-iron and about off the right heel with a 9-iron. With the driver you hit the teed-up ball an ascending blow, the club head having already passed its lowest point. With the short irons you hit it a descending blow, taking a good-sized divot after the ball.

How far away do you stand? Again the same principles apply throughout. You 'measure off', as before, with the left arm extended, and yourself poised and in balance, though naturally stooping a little more with the shorter clubs than you did with the driver.

Thomson also likes to have his feet progressively closer together as the shots become shorter. It all seems to fit into a very simple and intelligible pattern. As the shots become short enough to require judgment rather than power for their execution, he likes to open the stance slightly, drawing his left foot back a little.

For the short game his maxim, typically, is that one should always look for the *simplest* way. He describes the high wedge shot, which we so much admire when played by professionals, as, for most people, 'a form of lunacy'. The more you can picture a short approach as a kind of extended putt, he says, the better.

The ruin of most handicap players' short game comes from their efforts to hit the ball *up*. It is the golfer's job to hit it *forwards*, the lofted club's job to hit it *upwards*. It is an old professional trick, in trying to teach this to beginners, to put a lofted club into their hands and invite them to try to hit the ball along the ground into a bunker between them and the flag. They concentrate on hitting the ball forwards, whereupon it sails over the bunker.

Thomson is a supremely good bunker player. Perhaps his finest exhibition of this art was when he won the Open at Lytham, where they have innumerable bunkers, of which he encountered at least his share. I have always remembered his remark afterwards that he had 'never seen such beautiful sand'. He sincerely regards 'splashing' the ball out of sand as the simplest shot in the whole game, if only because there is so much greater a margin for error than with a similar shot off grass.

'The chief factor is the club itself. There are some atrocious old sand-irons about that even Snead could not play with. You want one with a wide sole, with the back edge considerably lower than the front.' He thinks little or nothing of most of the so-called 'dual purpose' clubs.

He reckons to stand well behind the ball and to 'measure off' carefully to the exact point that he wishes to hit the sand. Instead of hitting the ball first and the turf afterwards, you hit the sand first and the ball afterwards. You can hit the sand anything from two to six inches behind and it may well be sometimes that the club-face never actually touches the ball at all. So far as you are concerned at any rate, you are playing a shot at the sand rather than at the ball. His only golden rule is 'swing very slowly'.

Thomson is also—again in an unostentatious and 'simple' way—a supremely good putter. I spent a long time drawing him out on the subject and from this I think three main points emerge. He does not think that the grip matters unduly—indeed he used the words 'almost any grip will do'—but he has no doubt about his own method.

To initiate it, take a normal grip, then rotate your left hand to the left so that the back of it is at about 45 degrees to the ground; do likewise with your right hand to the right, and then stick your right thumb firmly on the shaft. He also reckons to stand with his eyes vertically over the ball. All this is common ground but there are many who might vastly improve by giving it a trial.

His second point interested me because I have so often referred to it as one of the main secrets of Locke's phenomenally successful putting and because it is something that we can all so easily do and, even when we mean to, so often don't. It is to carry out a sort of *drill* : in other words, to find a set of motions that suits our own particular eye and temperament and carry them out, without exception, every time we putt.

Locke's drill will be familiar to all who have seen him either in person or on the television : two practice strokes, a step up to the ball, one look at the hole and away it goes. Even with 'this to tie for the Open' this drill never varies.

For his third point I quote Thomson's own words. 'It must incorporate some sort of *determined tap*. What kills putting is the old so-called "stroking" method. You don't stroke a putt like you stroke a cat. If you do, it is usually timid and damned lucky if it goes in the hole. The most natural way is to give it a tap, like a child instinctively does.

'None of the people who follow through like poor old . . . (and here he named four distinguished players who shall remain anonymous, two British and two Americans) . . . have ever really been any good on the greens.' He named as the world's best putters Rosburg, Casper, Ford, Palmer and Venturi—all Americans who hit the ball with a firm tap rather than a smooth stroking movement. This, I need hardly add, is not to be confused with a quick jerk or jab!

Like Locke, Thomson thinks it essential to hold the club loosely with a very light, sensitive grip and likes to have the *feeling* that he is playing the same stroke every time, increasing the length more by lengthening the backswing than by hitting harder.

I believe all good putters, and the rest of us during our days 'on', have this feeling, though whether we are any longer capable of a 'very light sensitive grip' remains to be proved. I did not have the heart to ask him the $64,000 question 'How, if at all, can you cure the "jitters"?' After all, he was due next day to play in the Open Championship. Anyway, he would not have known. He is only thirty and has never had them!

Finally two postscripts. Some time ago Thomson put his thoughts on golf on to a long playing record, and I think it excellent. The number is 33SX 1068. Secondly, I am told by a friend that he is desperately anxious to get hold of an original Braid-Mills aluminium putter with a hickory shaft. Has anyone got one in the attic? If so, I shall be delighted to pass it on.[1]

---

[1] This resulted in 105 offers from readers and I duly passed one on. After all that, I am not sure that Thomson really did want one!

10.53 to the Devil's Dyke

I join in congratulating *Golf Illustrated* on attaining this week its seventieth birthday. Three score years and ten of golf! Though I am privileged to know characters like J. H. Taylor, eighty-nine; Willie Auchterlonie, eighty-eight; John Rowe, who at the age of ninety-two wrote me a three-page letter from Forest Row the other day in handwriting which cannot have been better when he was in his teens:[1] and the comparatively youthful Bernard Darwin, who at the time of the first issue had seven years to wait before he was to captain Cambridge, I scan the first volume, which I have before me as I write, as though looking into a different and in many ways, let it be whispered, better world.

No. 1. Vol. 1. Friday 19 September 1890. Price twopence. (No notice can be taken of anonymous communications) ... 'The extension of what has been justly termed the National Game of Scotland has made such rapid strides in the last few years that there is hardly a place of any notoriety in the British Islands, and in India and many of the Colonies, that does not boast its Golfing Green. ...'

Nevertheless, golf outside Scotland was in its infancy. It had begun to invade England, but Harry Vardon had yet to make the tours which were to spread it like a prairie fire across the United States. Lord Leconfield had just laid out

---

[1] See 'The Old Gutty-Puncher', page 247.

nine holes in his estate at Petworth; Lord Granville had had a nice little course laid out at Walmer Castle; some Bournemouth gentlemen had found a splendid stretch of gorse-covered moor at Brockenhurst.

The gallant 91st Division had started a thriving and popular club in the Happy Valley at Hong Kong and 'we are happy to hear that an attempt is being made to acquire the land between the boundary of the St. George's Club and Deal for the purpose of starting a new club, to be called the Cinque Ports Club. This will give an uninterrupted course of four miles straight on end. . . .'

Some of my own favourites, I note with a superior air, were already well established. 'The Brighton and Hove golf links are upon the Downs some four miles distant from the Metropole Hotel (at present Brighton's central attraction). After breakfast the golfer may stroll up to the main line station, catch the 10.53 train to the Devil's Dyke and, taking a return ticket for tenpence, find himself in the agreeable company of twenty or thirty golfers. . . . There is plenty of room for 18 holes and the sooner it is done the better.'

Now blackberries grow on the Dyke Railway, the Downs are ploughed up, and the extra nine holes they made have been sacrificed to the children of the neighbouring Council estate. Such is progress.

Eastbourne, too, was in full swing, but had been attacked somewhat contemptuously by a golfer from Fife. It was good enough, the secretary replies, for such as Horace Hutchinson, and this great figure bestrides the pages of 1890. Already twice champion, he wins the William IV medal at the Royal and Ancient, writes copiously, and has just produced the immortal Badminton volume, his presentation copy of which to his wife was in turn presented by her to me and is my most prized golfing possession.

John Ball wins the Open at Prestwick with two rounds of 82, and two professionals, Willie Fernie and Archie Simpson, three strokes behind, divide the first and second prizes of £13 and £6. After them, Willie Park and Andrew Kirkaldy divide a fiver.

Even in 1890, however, the game is already on its way to ruin. 'An Old Golfer,' complaining of the complexity of the Rules, reduces them to four (sixty-nine years later I managed to do it in 10!) 'I have nothing to say about medal play, which is bastard and not true Golf,' he adds. 'Those who go for it must make their own laws—ludicrous mostly.'

And, as a final touch, the very first letter in No. 1. Vol. 1. signed 'One of the Old School' is headed, believe it or not, 'Ought the stimy to be abolished?' The controversy went steadily on for another sixty years and every scribbler on golf shed a tear when it died.

Would you put back the golfing clock if you could? Would you go out in your knickerbockers, subject to possible ridicule, and hand your seven clubs to a skinny little boy called Taylor at Westward Ho!, at 6d. a round, minus 3d. if you lost a ball? I know one thing, I would take the 10.53 to the Devil's Dyke tomorrow!

The Maestro

When anyone asks me who is the greatest striker of a golf
ball I ever saw, my answer is immediate. It is Henry Cotton.
I am just old enough to have seen Harry Vardon play, but
was not old enough at the time to make a fair assessment of
his powers. Whatever they were, I cannot believe them to
have been greater than Cotton's in the 'thirties. He lifted up
the nation's golfing spirit after eleven long years of American
domination and, with it, the status of his own profession.

For this the Americans themselves were largely responsible.
In 1928, when he was twenty-one, he set sail for the United
States under his own steam, buying his own ticket and taking
with him a letter of credit for £300, which incidentally he
brought home intact. He soon appreciated that the great
sporting figures of the day were regarded in America almost
as the aristocracy, whereas at home sport carried with it no
special standing. When Walter Hagen came to England to
win our championships, he stayed at the Savoy and drove up
to the course in a hired Rolls-Royce. He was already 'one up'
on the rest of the field. Cotton decided that what Hagen
could do he could do.

I think it is fair to say that Cotton regarded himself, in his
competitive days, as a kind of 'property', to be taken the
greatest care of and kept in the best possible condition if
it were to give the desired results. For this reason he took it

to the best hotels and at lunch time, having no desire for the smoky air and, for the celebrated, the inevitable attachment of bores and sycophants to be found in the club-house, he changed his clothes in the car and retired to the hotel. Naturally enough, there were those who thought he regarded himself as too good for the common herd.

'I believe,' he told me the other day, 'that I was one of only about four professionals at that time to have a car at all. Arthur Havers had one, I remember, and another professional in the north of England. It was hardly "done" for a golf pro to own a car.' His own was one of those vast Mercedes with ironmongery sprouting from the bonnet and he used to strengthen his hands by driving it with one hand. As against that, he was roundly abused for declining, when he came upon a woman motorist stranded on the road, to crank her car. One backfire could have ruined the 'property'.

He developed an immense strength in his hands, and they became the focal point in his essentially simple swing. As the ball flew straight at the flag, you felt that, if you hit it in that fashion, it could hardly do anything else. He could do almost anything with a golf ball on purpose and would have made a great trick-shot artist. We often used to challenge him to take his driver from a bad lie on the fairway, simply for the aesthetic pleasure of seeing the ball fly away as though fired from a rifle, and I remember once at Bad Ems seeing him knock a shooting stick out of the ground with a 1-iron shot at a range of 20 yards. We christened him the Maestro, and he deserved it.

At the same time he developed a flair for getting himself into the news, sometimes, but not always, on purpose. With all this he was naturally the centre of attraction wherever he played, and became probably the first professional golfer to be recognizable at once to the man in the street.

In 1929, now aged twenty-two, Cotton played in his first Ryder Cup match at Leeds, where he beat Al Watrous by 4 and 2, and it now seemed only a matter of time before he won the championship. He had his chances, but on at least two occasions let them slip, mainly, as he now thinks, through listening to the rumours that used to fly about the course before the present walkie-talkie system came into use, and not appreciating what he needed to do.

It was against this background that the championship opened at Sandwich in 1934. Cotton had with him four sets of clubs—why, I do not know—and for once could not hit his hat with any of them. He practised on Saturday till darkness drove him in, and had never been in such discouraging form. He settled on a set of clubs, for better or for worse, and on Monday morning, in the first qualifying round, was drawn to go out first, accompanied by a marker. He played what remains in his own opinion the best round of his life. He hit every green in the right number—33 shots, 33 putts; total 66. Such is golf.

The magic lasted. He opened the championship proper with a 67, and in such a way that one saw no reason why he should ever again take more. On the second day he arrived on the 17th tee needing only two par fours for another 67 and the then fantastic total of 134. At each hole he hit a tremendous drive. His second to the seventeenth ruled the flag and finished about 12 feet from the hole, and he holed the putt for a 3. He hit another magnificent iron shot to the last hole, though he cannot have seen it finish, for he was at once enveloped by a stampeding multitude determined to see history being made on the last green.

I remember the shot perfectly. It bounced a couple of times and came quietly to rest about four feet from the stick. He made no mistake with the putt and history had indeed been made. Sixty-five! A total of 132 and the nearest man, Alfred Padgham, nine strokes behind.

On the morning of the final day Cotton turned in a 72 in harder conditions, a more than adequate score which was beaten by only three players, and now he was out on his own by 12 strokes. He returned to his hotel for lunch in the usual way, and I do not believe it entered the head of a single person present that they might be about to witness in the afternoon the most agonizing golfing spectacle any can remember to this day.

Things went instantly wrong. He timed his arrival for the start but found it postponed for a quarter of an hour owing to the immense crowd which had assembled to watch the triumphant formality of his final round. In his own words: 'Like a fool, I went and sat in a small tent all by myself. Lack of experience again. Today I should go out and hit balls, go for a walk, anything bar sit and brood. Already I had been undermined by people congratulating me before I had won. The editor of one of the golf magazines seemed to think he had appointed himself my official manager and kept popping in and out of lunch telling me not to sign anything without consulting him when I had won. I had been humbled by golf too often. I sat and thought how anyone could take 82 in a championship, and anyone else could do 69, and there is the whole thing gone. Why, it was only a mile or two away, at Deal, that poor Abe Mitchell took 83 to George Duncan's 71 and lost 12 strokes and the championship in a single round.'

The start was a foretaste of what was to come, and I hardly like to write of it even now. His first drive was skied and his second with a 2-iron hit a lady, standing at cover point, on the knee. Through the green it is no exaggeration to say that a competent 12-handicap player would have given him a good game and, if he had not putted, considering the circumstances, miraculously, he might have taken 90.

There was much talk at the time of his having eaten something that disagreed with him or having failed to digest his modest lunch. The latter, I am sure, is true or he could not speak of it with such feeling to this day. 'I played in a cold sweat and wanted to be sick. I ought to have gone off and vomited in the nearest hedgerow, but I didn't, partly because I was too ashamed and partly because there aren't any hedgerows at St. George's anyway. I could not get anything but fives. I could not get a 4 even at drive-and-pitch holes where all the week I had been looking for threes.'

At the long thirteenth—'another b—— 5 coming'—the course of the round, and with it, he now agrees, probably of his life, was changed. He holed a four-yard putt for 4. It broke the spell and he coasted home to win by five shots from Sid Brews, of South Africa. He missed a short putt on the last green but it did not matter now. A British player had won the championship at last and they carried him shoulder high off the green.

Nevertheless, his real turn was yet to come. Although the Americans had won for eleven successive years, he had not really beaten them, for, with the exception of the ageing Macdonald Smith, none of them was there. Three years later all of them were.

Having won the Ryder Cup match at Southport by seven matches to three, the American team, illuminated by such names as Nelson, Snead, Sarazen, Horton Smith and, for good measure, the non-playing captain, Hagen, proceeded to Carnoustie for the Open. This is the toughest of all the championship courses, and in 1937 it bore little resemblance to the Carnoustie on which Hogan was to win in 1953.

The eighteenth, for instance, was a drive and a wooden club against the mere 7- or 8-iron in Hogan's year, and the weather was uniformly foul. Cotton started steadily with 74, 72, 73, which left him three shots behind Reginald Whitcombe, one behind Reginald's brother Charles, and two ahead of Charles Lacey, who had long since emigrated from this country to America.

For the final round the heavens opened. The rain made such a din upon the Press tent as to drown completely the clatter of the typewriters within, while green-keepers were summoned frantically from green to green to 'squeegee' the water away and keep them fit for play. Cotton's main memory of the final round is of his efforts to keep his powder dry, in other words his hands and the grips of his clubs. He had several left-hand gloves, which he took off whenever possible and changed when wet, and a series of towels hanging under his umbrella. To the layman non-golfer this may not sound a particularly difficult operation, but in fact it is. Furthermore, once you have lost the battle, nothing can retrieve it.

He then set about using the rain to his advantage . . . 'I

was young enough to pitch deliberately in the right puddle, even from quite a distance away. I picked the puddle nearest to the flag and used it as a brake to stop the ball.' As a measure of this accuracy, he in fact got round with only 29 putts, which to anyone who was present must still seem hard to believe.

He came to the last hole, with the intertwining Burn and, on the left, the out-of-bounds fence, where poor Jose Jurado had lost the Open sixteen years before, needing a 6 to beat Reginald Whitcombe, who, like his brother, had finished with what seemed in the circumstances a very respectable 76 . . . 'I hit a huge drive, found it in a bad lie and had only one thought in my head: "Not over the fence. Not over the fence". So I played at the bunker on the right. If I hooked it, it was on the green. If I hit it straight, it was still in play.'

He hit it perfectly, into the bunker. Again only one thought: 'Mustn't skim it out over the fence'. He played safe and was down in 5 for a 71, beating poor Whitcombe, whom I so well remember watching being photographed on the practice putting green as the winner, by two strokes, and the nearest American Ryder Cup player by six. This final round, though it had none of the drama of his 65 or of the dreadful anticlimax at Sandwich, remains in my mind as the finest I have ever seen in a championship.

Fourteen years after winning his first championship, in 1948, Cotton won his third. King George VI came to Muirfield to watch the play and it seemed typical of Cotton that he should hole the course for the King's benefit in 66.

'Bernardo'

It seems almost unbelievable that Bernardo, otherwise Mr. Bernard Darwin, C.B.E. (for 'services to literature and sport') is no longer with us. He has died at the age of eighty-five and, as he took to writing about golf in his early twenties and continued almost to the day of his death, there are few indeed who can remember the game without his pen and its influence in the background.

He wrote lives of Dickens, W. G. Grace and John Gully, the prize-fighter; children's books; innumerable fourth leaders for *The Times*, which could be detected by the faithful within a few lines; and an annual account of the University sports until, being a fervent Cambridge man, he was 'relieved of office for too gross a partiality'. But his principal love was golf.

He took it as a case of 'divinity shaping our ends'. His uncle joined the King's Regiment; therefore, he was quartered in Liverpool; therefore, he was introduced to golf —at Formby; therefore, during his leave he created the course at Aberdovey, borrowing some flower pots for the holes; therefore, his nephew was in turn introduced to golf and 'took passionately to the game at the age of eight'.

John Beck recalls hearing, as a young man, Herbert Asquith say to his father: 'I consider Bernard Darwin to be the greatest living essayist in the English language.' Another eminent critic described him as one of the six best essayists since Charles Lamb.

If the standard of writing about golf is at least as high as in other games, as I like to think it is, this is due very largely to the fact that Bernardo was ever present as a model, not only in his writing but in his fairness and accuracy.

This does not mean that he was uncritical. In conversation he could be positively withering, but in his writings he conveyed the sense that golf was a pleasant game played in pleasant places by, on the whole, pleasant people—'the bravest, stupidest race in the world, the unconvincible, inextinguishable race of golfers'.

'It is not a crime to play a bad shot,' he once wrote, 'and the player may yet be a good husband and a good father and a true Christian gentleman.' Thus, when he did criticize, the blow went home. I remember that, many years ago, he was rather 'beastly' about a suburban club's course on which some tournament was played. It nearly broke their hearts.

He had, of course, been no mean player in his day. He captained Cambridge and won a Walker Cup single in America, having gone there to report the match and taken the place of a player who fell ill. He won the Worplesdon foursomes in partnership with the then Miss Joyce Wethered, reduced by an uncontrollable twitch to putting with his mashie, which he held farther and farther down the shaft as the tournament went on. His daily accounts of their progress, with Miss Wethered's partner 'lifting his venerable head', are remembered to this day.

Bernardo had one, to me, most amiable weakness. He allowed the game, and sometimes his partners, to make him very, very cross indeed. Quite my favourite story of him concerns his start in the Medal at Woking. At the first hole he laid his second shot a yard from the hole—and missed the putt. At the second, longish a short hole over a valley, he played an exquisite cut-up shot with a spoon—and missed a tiny putt for a two. At the third he missed yet another short one and was heard to be muttering darkly as he made his way to the 4th tee.

Here with the railway on the right and a central bunker bisecting the fairway into two narrow lanes, and a tricky sloping green, the champion himself is happy enough with a four. Bernardo put his second shot two feet from the hole. In a pregnant silence he missed the putt.

Brandishing his putter aloft and casting his eyes upward to the sky, he is alleged to have cried '*And now, God, perhaps You are satisfied!*'

Once, all square at the sixteenth in a foursome at Rye, he completely fluffed a very short putt. Instead of gesticulating on the spot, he turned on his heel and marched in silence to the distant rough. Here, banging his club repeatedly on the ground, he was heard to be muttering 'Why do I *play* this —— game? I do *hate* it so!'

He loved it, of course—if not in some of its modern forms. He was an inveterate practiser—not I think, with a view to improving his game but rather to be alone with a club and a ball and his thoughts. 'It is only in solitude,' he wrote, 'and preferably in the dusk when the lights begin to glimmer in the surrounding houses, that practice is truly heavenly and the nearest possible approach to the great defiant secret may be discovered.'

One of my bedside bibles is a book called *What Life Has Taught Me*, to which Bernardo was one of twenty-five distinguished contributors. He concluded his reflections with 'to spend a good part of your life doing the thing you happen to like best, in pleasant places and in pleasant company, seems to me to be not unenviable. I am afraid I would do it all over again.'

If only he could!

'I Played My Game, Sir'

A chorus of congratulation will, I am sure, be rising all over the golfing world for J. H. Taylor, the last of the 'great triumvirate', who is ninety today (1961). He is one of the two professionals who are honorary members of the Royal and Ancient, and Lord Cohen, the present captain, has sent him a silver salver bearing his own signature and that of every living past captain. These include, pre-war, the Duke of Windsor (1922) and Bernard Darwin (1934), and every captain since the war.

The gift, writes Lord Cohen, is a 'token of our affection for you personally and of our admiration for all that you have done for the game of golf'. I cannot help feeling that every club captain, on appreciating the occasion, may wish to send the great man a telegram. The address is 23, Windmill Lane, Northam, Devon, and the post office tell me they deliver on Sundays.[1]

Below his bungalow, on the flat expanse of land they call the 'Burrows', lies the links of Westward Ho!, where he began more than eighty years ago as a caddie boy, eventually to become President of the Club.

When he took to golf as his career professionals were a

[1] This produced so gratifyingly large an avalanche of telegrams that J. H. was shown on television sorting them all out.

rough and ready crowd, and it was probably J. H. more than any other single person who was responsible for rallying them together in the early days of the Professional Golfers' Association and starting them on the road to their present standing and prosperity.

Though he was renowned for his pitching with the mashie, what he really excelled in was the straightness of his long shots to the green—in days when holes, which today are nonchalantly dismissed with a drive and a 7-iron, required a drive and a brassie. They used to say of him that his only hazards were the direction posts.

One such shot—his cleek to the sixth, or Briars, at Hoylake, in the last of his five open championships in 1913—has been immortalized by the writers of the day. A. C. Croome said, 'It seemed to make a hole through the wind as it bored its way along.' Bernard Darwin wrote, 'The wind and the rain were terrific, but not so terrific as Taylor, with his cap pulled down, buffeting his way through them. . . . I can still see him, standing on rock-like feet, glued flat on the turf, watching that ball as it whizzes over the two cross bunkers straight for the green. There never was such a cleek shot; there never will be such another as long as the world stands.'

'Flat-footed golf, sir,' J. H. himself used to call it. 'Flat-footed golf.' He has the club with which he played that celebrated stroke in his sitting-room today.

Two of the pictures on his wall represent an achievement which may, I suspect, have given him almost as much satisfaction as his championships. One shows him with the late King when he was Duke of York, the other with the then Prince of Wales when they came successively to open the Duke's and Prince's courses in Richmond Park. J. H. was virtually the founder of these public courses and the hundreds who will be enjoying the fruits of his labours there today should lift their hats on the 1st tee in his honour.

How much golf would have lost if J. H. had achieved his original ambition to be a soldier or a sailor! He would not, in those days, have been able to reach the heights to which his character and ability would have taken him today. But, as Mr. Darwin has put it, it is certain that all who served with him would have remembered him.

As it was, the man who was to fire brassie shots to the distant flag as no man has fired them since was turned down because of his eyesight! Yet perhaps they were right, for it was his eyesight that eventually forced him to give up golf. I remember asking him some years ago whether he still played a few occasional holes. 'There's no point in hitting it,' he said, 'if you've got to get someone to tell you where it has gone.'

Looking back on his four score years and ten, J. H. may say of his life, as he once said after being defeated by a particularly brilliant display by Harry Vardon, 'I played my game, sir. I played my game.'

'No More Blind than You Are'

Two very considerable figures passed from the golfing scene last week, the first, of course, being J. H. Taylor, five times Open Champion and a member with Vardon and Braid of the 'Great Triumvirate'. For many years we had exchanged telegrams on our birthdays, his being on 19 March and mine on 18 March. Together with St. Patrick on the 17th, he once said, he thought we could consider ourselves a good mixed trio.

I have quoted previously his remark, on being beaten by a particularly brilliant display of Harry Vardon's, 'I played my game, sir. I played my game'. This could be said with abundant truth also of Critch, in other words Brig.-Gen. A. C. Critchley, C.M.G., C.B.E., D.S.O.—and what a game he played! Thinking back over the many qualities which made him unique to all who knew him well, I think that perhaps outstanding was his sheer zest for life, which throughout his time equalled that of a man twenty years younger.

Perhaps it sprang from his early life on the family ranch at Calgary where he and his brother, hugely enjoying themselves, 'grew up without the slightest benefit of education. We could hardly write and only just read. On the other hand, we could saddle ponies, ride for miles across the ranges, find our way in the dark without compasses, make our own camp and ride herd'. His impact at the age of nine on a small preparatory school at Eastbourne may well be imagined.

In 1918, after three years in France, he had risen to command Strathcona's Horse when he was asked to take over the new initial training command of the Royal Flying Corps, in which they were killing nearly 50 per cent of the cadets during flying training. One of his proudest possessions was a picture of a march-past, with himself, a slim ultra-military figure, straight as a ramrod and a brigadier general at twenty-seven, standing behind King George V and, leading the column, the future King George VI.

Next day the King wrote to his son, 'I was quite delighted with my visit to you last Friday and I must say General Critchley is a wonderful man, the very man for the job. Tell him from me that I never saw such keen boys as his cadets and I thought his system of training quite first rate and that I consider his by far the best training establishment that I have seen.'

Just before the Second World War Critch was back in the R.A.F. again—'Pilot Officer, Acting Air Commodore'—commandeering with bustling urgency the same sites in which this time he was to train aircrew in tens of thousands and to see them in turn inspected and commended by King George VI.

Critch then, at vast cost to himself since he had to sell his commercial interests, became Director-General of B.O.A.C. —incidentally turning a loss of nearly £2½ million into a profit of £1½ million, though not without causing a good deal of gnashing of teeth—and he could fairly claim to have been the 'discoverer' and founder of London Airport.

It is ironical that despite all his public service Critch will probably be best remembered for creating the sport of greyhound racing in this country, which all began through the late Charlie Munn showing him a picture of some dogs racing in Oklahoma. Since whippet racing was popular in the north, they started up in Manchester and for the opening evening printed 20,000 programmes. Two thousand people turned up.

Soon, a local bank manager was tiding them over with a positively final £5,000. For this he nearly got the sack—since which time the G.R.A. have put more than £100 million through his bank.

I first met Critch in 1931 when, as captain of the Cambridge team, I found myself due to play against him in the singles at Coombe Hill. 'Which,' I remember saying, 'is General Critchley?' I had been looking for a comparatively elderly figure with perhaps a white moustache. Instead, there was pointed out to me a virile, almost sergeant-major-like figure of about forty, handicap plus-one, taking savage practice swings at the daisies.

Possibly because I had the impertinence to beat him on the last green, Critch appeared to take to me and later we were to travel tens of thousands of miles together, in America, the Bahamas, Nigeria, the Far and Middle East and all over the Continent. Some of this was done in a vehicle of Black Maria aspect, and of his own design, known as 'Critch's caravan'. The driver sat by himself in front. Behind were two seven-foot sofas, a desk, a wireless, a bar and a sort of 'hall' for coats, clubs and general clobber. It remains the most comfortable road vehicle in which I have ever travelled.

As a golfer Critch was neither stylist nor theorist, but he was a tremendous match player and must have beaten innumerable players who would have ranked above him in the book of form. He won the Dutch, Belgian and Surrey Championships; the King William IV Medal at St. Andrews; and with his wife, Diana, the French mixed foursomes six times. Henry Cotton once told him he was 'the best second-class golfer in the world'.

Ten years ago, suddenly and without notice, Critch went blind, and this indeed confirmed what a tremendous man he was. Within a year he had entirely adjusted his life. 'Seventy-five per cent of the time,' he used to say, 'I am no more blind than you are.'

He continued to travel all over the world—to America, Australia, South Africa, and four times to Canada—and to conduct his business in London. He built himself a bungalow, where with his talking-machine he discovered the pleasures of literature and read five hundred books in ten years.

Critch will not have been afraid of dying. He was convinced that he had met Death before, during the illness which caused his blindness. He spoke to me vividly about it soon afterwards. Later he wrote: 'I felt that I was being forced backward, step by step. Behind me was Death, not a condition of the body but a person who spoke to me. I knew that he was a pleasant, decent man, and there was no need for me to be afraid of him. He did not call me Critch, but he seemed an old enough friend to do so if he wished. He said, "Don't worry. I'll look after you." '

Other voices, perhaps his own thoughts, said, 'If you give another inch, you've had it,' and he returned to the land of the living. Now death has won.

'Ex-Cambridge Triple Blue'

If you qualify to become a 'character' by having innumerable stories told about you in your own lifetime—this may be as good a definition as any—then my old friend and Halford Hewitt partner, John Morrison, was certainly a 'character'. He must also have been one of the outstanding all-rounders of his generation. In the changed social and economic climate of our times such a man simply could not 'happen' today.

In the papers he was inevitably tagged ' J. S. F. Morrison, the ex-Cambridge triple Blue'. In brief, he got a cricket and soccer Blue for the University before the 1914 war and a golf Blue after it, when he returned also to captain the cricket team. In the interval he flew elementary bombers from Italy and his name was among the eight who were awarded the very first D.F.C.s.

Younger people today can hardly imagine the impact made upon football in the 'twenties by that happy band of brothers known as The Corinthians. To any soccer-playing boy like myself their names were household words—Chadder, Knight, Hegan, Ashton, Doggart, Creek and, especially, that unsurpassed defensive trio, Bower and Morrison, at back, and Howard Baker in goal.

I remember vividly the suspense of waiting for the result of their great Cup-tie with Blackburn Rovers and the jubilation when we learned of their victory. I never knew, until Bower told me last week, that Morrison was captain on that historic occasion.

At other times he turned out for Sunderland, under the captaincy of Charles Buchan. Massive, fit and fearless, John was a law unto himself and I well remember Buchan telling me how he was allowed a special ration of a quart of beer before taking the field, and a quart at half-time.

By the time I came to know him he would have been in his forties and had already become something of an eccentric. When I was first selected for the Carthusian team at Deal, the captain craftily put Morrison and myself, as a blend of youth and experience, to play in the bottom foursome—and there we stayed for six hilarious years.

These six years, during which Charterhouse won the tournament five times, form the richest memory of my own golfing life. I not only played with Morrison in every match, but I also shared the same bedroom with his half-brother, that gay cavalier of golf, Dale Bourn—a combination, as you may imagine, not lightly to be forgotten.

I often thought that the good fortunes of the old firm of Morrison and Longhurst—it is fair to record that we were beaten only once in six years—was due as much as anything to the effect of my partner on opponents who had not seen him play before. He carried, in a torn canvas bag, a selection of clubs unmatched (in both senses) in golf.

Some had steel shafts, some had hickory. Many had handles as thick as a cricket bat's. He generally appeared in a deerstalker hat and a huge teddy-bear coat done up with string round the middle, which reduced him to something like a quarter swing, and, when it rained, he produced a vast waterproof skirt instead of trousers. It was nothing for him to take a putter from 60 yards.

It would not, I think, be uncharitable to say that my old partner tended, like so many of us, to be 'better after lunch'. It was with some foreboding, therefore, that I set out with him one morning at about 7.20 a.m., with the Goodwin Sands lightship still flashing, rather than hooting, in the

Channel. At the second hole he hit our second shot, with an evil-looking brassie, straight through a perishing cold head-wind to within ten feet of the flag. Arnold Palmer could not have done it better.

Before anyone could find the appropriate comment for this extraordinary and unexpected stroke, Morrison had looked at his watch and cried, 'Seven forty!'

At the same hole, after an excellent lunch, I drove our ball into a bird's-nest lie in the rough. When I got up to it, I found Morrison and his caddie tugging at his brassie, one at each end, like two chickens with a worm. 'No, no, sir!' the caddie was saying, to which Morrison was replying 'Yes, yes. It's teed up.' He hit it four yards.

Now he is no longer with us, but for those who knew him in his heyday his memory will never fade.

Oxford v Cambridge

University golf today is overshadowed by televised open championships, matches against the Americans, professionals playing for thousands of pounds, and all the clatter and babel of golf as a highly publicized game.

Yet the University match started seven years before the Amateur Championship and, until the outbreak of the last war, past Oxford and Cambridge players remained perhaps the most predominant single element in amateur golf.

Horace Hutchinson, who played top for Oxford in the first match in 1878, was runner-up in the first unofficial Amateur Championship in 1885, and won it in the following two years when it had been recognized as such, and the thread continued unbroken until 1940.

The first match, four-a-side and played by holes up or down, was won by Oxford by 24–0, W. T. Linskill, to whom I had always looked up piously as the 'founder of Cambridge golf', contributing 12 holes towards their defeat. He continued for many years to attach himself to Cambridge golf and golfers and seems, alas, to have been a slightly preposterous figure.

Oxford, to quote that spirited writer, A. C. Croome, principal founder of the Oxford and Cambridge Golfing Society, played on 'the marshiest part of Cowley marsh, where a few hedges and here and there a cricket pavilion served to lend interest to the game'. Cambridge played on Coldham Common, 'where the chief hazards were the abominable lies through the green and a poisonous smell emitted by some glue works'.

Bernard Darwin, who played for Cambridge in 1885 and 1886 and was captain in the following year, remembers it for its ditches, 'haunted by ruffians who stamped your ball into the mud'.

In those days Cambridge, instead of travelling up and down the country in motor-cars to celebrated clubs every Saturday and Sunday, played the Old Cantabs, Felixstowe and Yarmouth home and away, and Royston and Biggleswade, who 'weren't much good'. When they played Oxford on Wimbledon Common in 1896—largely because Linskill, who had appointed himself a kind of permanent secretary, said he could not afford to go to Sandwich—they travelled from King's Cross in a horse charabanc, complete with piper. Linskill, for whom the piper, the celebrations and the suspense of a halved match had proved something of a strain, travelled back in the boot.

Linskill's last playing year was 1882, when, as Croome recorded in 1913, 'he could not hold Ludovic J. Grant, who now presides over the affairs of Edinburgh University, the Royal and Ancient Golf Club of St. Andrews and other minor institutions in Scotland'.

Lord Russell of Killowen used to tell a story which indicates how limited were the Universities' golfing resources in those days. He was sitting in his rooms at Oxford one evening when the captain came in and said: 'Do you play golf? One of our fellows is injured.' 'No, I am afraid I don't.' 'What a pity! If you had, I would have asked you to play against Cambridge tomorrow.' Oxford turned up one short, the only time, I believe, in the history of the match.

In 1904 there occurred at Woking an incident which is remembered to this day. Coming to the last hole both C. C. Wedderburn (Oxford) and C. H. Alison (Cambridge), who was later to become one of the outstanding golf architects of his time, each hit his ball on to the club-house roof. Oxford, naturally, were lucky enough to bounce back but the Cambridge ball remained stuck in the roof.

The first ladder proved too short but Alison, persisting in the true tradition of playing the ball where it lies, found one 'less deficient in loft', climbed up, 'found his ball lying slightly cupped on a flat sheet of lead and played a beautiful pitch to within four yards of the hole'. Alas, he missed the putt.

A few years later University golf closed down for the war. How many were killed who might have played thereafter no man can say. When they resumed in 1920, nearly every man on both sides had returned from battle of some kind.

Oxford started with three resounding names—Wethered, Tolley, M.C., Beck, M.C.—the first two destined to become Amateur Champions, Beck to captain the only successful British Walker Cup team in history.

In the meantime Cambridge golf was being revived by C. P. Johnstone, a man of exceptional modesty who had had a bullet through the lung at Ypres and has been described to me as 'probably the best captain ever'.

The first post-war golf match was played nine-a-side by singles only, at Sunningdale, and was the last, though two renegade Cambridge captains of the 1930s are alleged to have made similar suggestions, to be played on an inland course.

A legend has persisted—and I confess to having been brought up on it myself—that Cambridge 'fiddled the order', but this has no justification whatever in fact. Johnstone, as befits a captain—and so it should always be—played himself top and was then left with the problem of whom to put against Tolley, who was probably the best player in the country and was, indeed, to prove it in the Amateur Championship six weeks later.

Morrison had played four times for Cambridge, twice at No. 2 and twice at No. 4. 'His style is not graceful,' wrote Bernard Darwin at the time, 'and he does unorthodox things with his rather large body, but he has great power, a serene temperament and a capacity for holing doubtful putts.'

Johnstone decided that, while no one was likely to beat Tolley, this was the only one who conceivably might.

In the event, Tolley 'doing it all with such disgusting ease', went round in 70, equalling the then course record, and won easily enough. When I chanced on him recently—an impressive figure with, his friends may find it hard to believe, an upturned handlebar 'Kaiser' moustache—he confirmed with due modesty that Morrison was the man who might at that time have beaten him. So much for the legend. Suffice to add that Cambridge won by 9–3.

The longest individual match ever played in the series took place at Hoylake in 1927 between Raymond Oppenheimer and the Cambridge captain, Geoffrey Grimwade, of Australia. In a gale such that it took each of them four full shots to reach the third hole, they battled on to the forty-first, where Grimwade at last prevailed. As Cambridge had already won, it seemed a trifle pointless and from that day it was decided to abandon extra-hole matches and call a half a half.

Three years later Hoylake was the scene of perhaps the most extraordinary match of all, when all the bunkers filled with water. The two captains, Bob Baugh, of Alabama (Oxford) and Eric Prain (Cambridge), waited to the last moment and then, rather than adjourn to a neighbouring course, made up some local rules of their own.

I never quite knew what they were but my opponent, A. C. Marples, being the Oxford secretary, fortunately did and, though I shall go to my grave declaring that they worked to his advantage, I cannot attribute to them the margin by which he beat me.

At any rate, the storm that had filled the bunkers was nothing to the storm that broke on the heads of the luckless captains for daring to tamper with the sacred Rules of Golf. One critic even suggested that they would do the game a service by giving it up altogether! I could not understand such bitterness at the time and cannot now. It still seems most unfair.

Perhaps the most memorable individual match in the past thirty years was that between P. H. F. White (Cambridge), now Science Master at Harrow, and Cecil Middleton (Oxford) on the original Prince's, Sandwich, in 1933. Two down at lunch, White holed the first 14 holes, from the back tees in March, in 51 shots, or five under fours, and it is said that the only time Middleton spoke was to observe darkly, 'This course is meant to be done in fours, not threes'. A half was the only possible result.

A Bunch of Lousy Golfers

I was sorry indeed, on returning from America, to find that Archie Compston had died. I remember my first meeting with him as though it were yesterday. Cambridge University, of which I had at that time the honour to be captain, had gone to play a Sunday match against Coombe Hill and had been duly defeated. A tall, dominating and extremely handsome figure, he was sitting on the fender in front of the fire. 'You're just a bunch of lousy golfers,' he said—he pronounced it 'goffers'—'I could beat any three of you.'

Feeling that this could hardly be allowed to pass, N. A. Keith, W. H. Bermingham and I took him on. I thought we were on to a good thing and wagered accordingly, but the result came under the heading of 'Learning the Lessons of Life the Hard Way'. Archie saw to it that we went off the farthest back tees and there were six holes which, in winter, we could not reach in two and which he could, and did. He holed the course in 68 and beat us on the last green, and I had to sell my motor-car.

Gambling was high at Coombe Hill in those days and Archie, who could survey the course on any given day and be certain within a stroke or so of how many he would take to get round, reckoned to make anything up to a couple of thousand a year—equal to at least five today—from betting on his own matches.

The income tax people tried to tax him on it but he retorted that it was his own money and they wouldn't think of paying him if he lost. He took them to court and, to the general delight, won the match.

Later I rashly remarked in his hearing at Coombe Hill that I would give a fiver to anyone who could show me how to hook instead of slice. He hauled me straight out in rain and semi-darkness to his teaching hut and within minutes had me hooking them round my neck into the gorse. His terms were cash on the nail, he said—and I hope he paid tax on it.

Archie was then at the height of his powers. Two years previously in a 72-hole match against Walter Hagen he had pulverized that great player into a humiliating defeat by 18 and 17. Hagen, I fancy, did not care what happened on the second day, but he certainly did not mean to be 14 down at the end of the first.

Within months of my first meeting him, however, Archie Compston was to suffer an experience which, I always think, prevented him from then onwards from achieving the heights of which he was so obviously capable. In the third round of the 1930 Open at Hoylake a brilliant 68 had gained him six shots on Bobby Jones and he now led him, and the field, by a stroke. In the afternoon, disaster followed disaster and he took 82. It left its mark on him and he never looked like winning the Open again.

Archie was blunt, direct and forthright in both his ideas and his speech, and on occasion tactless and even rude. When some inoffensive club golfer came to him for a lesson, he was liable to gaze down from his great height at the man's clubs and yell to his club-maker in the next room, 'George, show this gentleman a proper set of golf clubs!'

If you survived the initial exchanges, however, and told him not to talk nonsense but get on with the job, he would throw his head back and roar with laughter, and you soon realized that under the rugged exterior he was just a great big, gentle, genial giant. He was the most inspiring teacher-cum-taskmaster I ever knew and I am sure that Pam

Barton, who won the British and U.S. Championships in the same year but was killed, alas, on service in the war, would have said the same.

I would give much to have been present when he was giving a lesson at the Mid-Ocean in Bermuda to Virginia, the then Marchioness of Northampton. So exasperated did she become with him that eventually she 'did' him on the shin with the sharp edge of an 8-iron. 'What did he do?' I asked. 'He bellowed and said to me, "Now you hit a golf ball",' she said.

I was, however, present on an occasion which was later preserved for posterity by Mel with a cartoon in *The Tatler*. A rather officious little man with eye-glass, long plus-fours and a squared-off sort of close haircut was holding forth to the company when Archie, about twice his height, rubbed the palm of his hand up and down on the top of his head and in his booming voice said, 'Gee, what a lie for a brassy'.

On another occasion, having missed a short putt in a tournament before the war at North Manchester, he overheard a boy sitting at the edge of the green saying: 'Cor. Do better myself!' Whereupon he strode over, yanked the wretched boy to his feet, paraded him on to the green, set down the ball, handed him the club and told him to get on with it. To his eternal credit the boy holed out—and no one laughed more loudly than Archie.

He was among the first of the 'showman golfers'. Women loved or loathed him—the former in the majority—and followed him round in flocks, but he never married. A lonely and, when you knew him, lovable man—ever searching for something he never quite found.

How Long is Five Minutes?

The experience of presiding over a golfing 'quiz' at the Shirley Park Club, Croydon, enables me to take yet another tilt at the manifest absurdity of many of the rules of golf. These occupy 93 pages of a pocket-sized booklet and the Decisions arising out of, presumably, their lack of clarity—since, if club committees could understand them, they would hardly need to write to the R and A for a decision—account for an ever-increasing file now about two inches thick.

I doubt whether there are half a dozen people in the country who could successfully back themselves to give a correct decision on every contingency in golf. Professionals playing for thousands of pounds seem often unable to interpret the simplest of rules and, when in doubt, sit down and refuse to budge till some luckless official has been summoned from the club-house to adjudicate.

This ludicrous situation—if you accept it as such—has arisen, I think, through the fact that, although it has always been accepted that you 'can't legislate for cheats', successive generations of golfing law-makers have in fact tried to do so.

No one, I am sure, is at heart keener to untangle the web of legislation which now surrounds the conscientious golfer than the Chairman of the Rules of Golf Committee, Mr. Gerald Micklem. Four years ago he produced in 'potted version' some guidance on the rules of golf, printed on a thing like a score-card and telling you and me all we normally need to know.

Every golfer really ought to have one of these in his bag, especially as they have the additional merit of costing nothing. Any club secretary can obtain one for each of his members simply by writing to the Golf Foundation, 2 St. James's Square, London, S.W.1.

Much of the rest of the rules is superfluous rubbish, or at any rate, when applied, results in rubbish—such as, for instance, the following question from our quiz. 'In a four-ball match the player's ball bounces off a tree that is out of bounds and hits one of the opponents who is still in bounds. Can the opponent's partner continue to play out the hole?'

The opponent's partner, mark you, has been walking quietly along, minding his own business. Yet the answer is 'No'. Both opponents are out of the hole. This was greeted with derisive disbelief, but the question-setter had the last word. He proved it by producing the book.

Here is another: 'In a stroke competition the competitor's ball strikes his own trolley, which at the moment is being courteously pulled along by his fellow competitor. Does he suffer two penalty strokes?' The answer is 'Yes', the assumption presumably being that, unless you impose a savage penalty for this obvious inadvertence, people will start doing it on purpose—though in the hope of what advantage heaven knows.

Some years ago I produced my own rules of golf for 'the club golfer who desires a common code and who has no intention of cheating', and I am still of the modest opinion that my Rule I is the best ever written. It reads: 'The game shall be played in the traditional manner and with as little delay as possible. Penalty: match play, loss of hole; stroke play, two strokes.'

This, of course, is equivalent to Section 40 of the Army Act. If they could not 'get' you under another rule, they could always do so under Section 40, the one about 'contrary to good order and military discipline'.

Thus, in my rules if you by mistake hit your own bag or

yourself or your opponent or his bag nothing happens—but if you do it on purpose you are 'got' by Rule I. You are not playing the game in the traditional manner.

I had passed the whole of my golfing life, till this week, under the impression that once you had deemed a ball lost and gone back to play another, you had 'had it'. Not so. If it is found within five minutes of starting the search for it, you can still play it—provided, of course, that you have not by now played another.

The five-minute rule is not itself strictly workable. Nobody stops to consult his watch on starting to look for a ball—nor should I willingly play again with an opponent whom I found to be timing me as I looked for mine. It is rather like catching a salmon. People will tell you that it took them 27 minutes to land it—but I have yet to meet the man who at the moment of first hooking a salmon turned to look at his watch.[1]

Nor can we be relied upon to estimate minutes any more than, in the old days, the expression 'within 20 yards of the flag' (which is still, I believe, retained by the Americans). I once went diving—not the 'skin' variety but helmet, lead boots and the lot. Shortly after immersion I began to pass out and was hauled ignominiously to the surface. I would have sworn in a court of law that I had been under water for approximately three minutes. The answer was twelve and a half.

A breath of common sense is beginning at last to find its way into the rules and from New Year's Day, 1964, you will be able to play a whole round with an extra club in your bag (quite by mistake and possibly not your own club anyway) and be fined only two holes in match play or four strokes in medal—instead of 18 holes or 36 points.

In my own rules this nonsense could not occur, as there is no limit to the number of clubs a man may be fool enough to carry.

My old friend the rule about 'testing the surface of the

[1] Nonsense, wrote a very senior R.A.F. officer by return of post. The very first thing he did was to look at his watch.

green' (penalty two strokes or loss of hole!) remains with us, and it was only during the Ryder Cup match at Atlanta this year that its purpose was explained to me by Mr. Joe Dey, who is the executive director of the U.S.G.A. and very learned in these matters. It appears that with nap on the greens, as in the U.S. and many Commonwealth countries, if every player rubs up the green to see which way the grass is growing, the result is a terrible mess.

Now that we have parted company with the U.S. on many rules, we could perhaps at the next revision start all over again and create a simple and intelligible set of our own, allowing us among other things to 'test the surface of the green', as we have all been doing for years.

The new rules could also perhaps cover the following, which defeated the panel the other day and is to be sent to the R and A for a decision. During a four-ball match a player about to putt asks one of the opponents how many strokes he has played, the opponent replies four and suddenly remembers that it is five. As the first player is about to putt the opponent does not like verbally to correct his statement as it would distract the player, so he gesticulates to the player's partner that it is five by holding up five fingers. Is the player's partner correct in similarly indicating that he has only played two?'[1]

---

[1] The then Chairman of Lloyds responded to this by sending me an excerpt from *The Times* report of a case before the Lord Chief Justice in which a lady appealed against her conviction for prostitution from a ground-floor window in Curzon Street.

'Her method was (1) to attract their attention to her by tapping on the window pane with some metal object as they passed by in the street in front of her, and (2), having so attracted their attention, to invite them in for a price which she indicated by extending three fingers of her hand and indicating the correct door of the premises. On one occasion the price so indicated by the appellant was agreed and the man entered the premises, leaving some 15 minutes later. On another occasion the price so indicated by the appellant was not agreed by the man concerned, who, in his turn, made a counter-proposal as to price by extending two fingers of his hand. That counter-proposal was not accepted by the appellant and the man walked away.'

'Indestructible—How Long?'

All too soon, since a year now seems to pass rather more quickly than did a single term at school, there comes the annual task of filling in the dates in the diary. 'The happy man,' Sir Winston has written, 'is he whose work and pleasure are one,' so it is with pleasure that I note that my work for the Open Championship will cause me to spend the second week in July at St. Andrews.

Few great links can have changed quite so much as the Old course and yet retain that quality which the golf architects call 'indestructibility', in other words when changes in balls, methods and equipment turn a good three-shot hole into a two-shotter, it remains a good two-shotter.

The course used to be no more than a narrow track about 40 yards wide cut through the whins, and not merely the same greens were used both out and coming home, as they are today, but also the same actual holes in the ground, one per green instead of two. Golf was regarded by the public as quite a dangerous game and I remember reading a book by one of the leading figures of the 'eighties and 'nineties that this was far from the truth and that he himself had 'only been struck twice this season'.

To what extent the Old course had widened out when the first of St. Andrews' nineteen open championships was played there ninety years ago (winner: Tom Kidd, with

179 for two rounds against a field of 26) I do not know, but I am sure that it possessed that same characteristic of making the player stop and think not merely 'what club is it?' but 'exactly what is it that I am trying to do?' Which makes it, to me, unique in its appeal today.

How long the Old course will remain 'indestructible' by forces like Nicklaus and the American-made small ball remains to be seen. I suppose that in the end it depends on the extent to which they water the approaches and the greens. Once you turn St. Andrews into 'target golf', it becomes to the mighty hitter just another pitch and putt course.

This has already, for the big fellows, destroyed most of the perils of the celebrated seventeenth, or Road Hole. Where previously they were terrified of going over into the road, they pitch nonchalantly up and leave themselves a putt for a three. Their real fear now is the fourteenth, where, from a tee used only in the championship, they have to drive about 240 yards into a narrow funnel bordered by the deep 'Beardies' bunkers on the left and the low out-of-bounds wall on the right. Both Locke and Thomson have taken seven here in the final round.

Long hitting in golf is a most mystifying affair, and nowhere more so than on the Old course. It seems to be perfectly well authenticated that in the summer of 1892 Ted Blackwell not only drove a gutty ball from the eighteenth to the steps of the club-house—about 390 yards—but also reached the fifth (520 yards) and the fourteenth (516 yards at that time—now 564) in two shots on the same day, these holes running exactly parallel with each other in opposite directions.

The ninth and tenth (359 and 314 yards today) are also in opposite directions and the other day I mentioned Eustace Storey, by no means a mighty hitter, having driven both in succession in the Walker Cup match of 1926. This brought reminiscences of the period from two other St. Andrews correspondents. One had played his second to the thirteenth (422 yards) and had walked over the ridge and down the other side, perhaps 300 yards from the tee, when a ball pitched clean over his head and finished in the bunker beside the green. The other, at the sixteenth (380 yards), had played out from the Deacon Sime bunker about 235 yards from the tee and was approaching his ball again, when he too was 'carried' from the tee—this time by another Walker Cup player, Eric McRuvie.

If, as I believe, these shots are simply not 'on' today for normal first-class players, what is the explanation? It has been suggested that the ball of the 'twenties went further than today. Dick Penfold, however, assures me that there is little difference; that today's ball goes, if anything, five or six yards further, and that the only great break-through in golf ball construction came with the invention, by his father, of the liquid-centred, tight-wound Maxfly in 1923.

The giant hitter—and, let it be added, the classical swinger—of those days was Cyril Tolley. Whenever one played a new course, the caddie was bound to say with awe, 'You should have seen where Mr. Tolley drove to, when 'e was 'ere,' thus rendering one's very best drive puny by comparison. It so happened that I ran into Tolley only a few evenings ago.

His mind, it seemed, was far removed from so trifling a pastime as golf. The only worthwhile game is, always will be, and probably always was—croquet. He aspires to be Champion of England—or was it Sussex?—within three years.

I drew him back eventually to the days when he was playing championships and Walker Cup matches at St. Andrews. Yes, he seemed to remember that during the week when he had played Bobby Jones in the semi-final in 1930 he had driven the last green at least three times, and without causing any great sensation. He remembered coming home on one occasion with a bit of wind behind and using nothing more than a niblick for his second—including the fourteenth and seventeenth.

Tolley thinks that many of the tees have been put back since that day and that the turf was firmer and drier. Perhaps this is true. I myself remember the Open of 1933 when the course was so burnt up that the ball left little puffs of dust as it bounced and Craig Wood drove into a bunker 420 yards from the 5th tee.

One of my earliest memories of golf is the drought of 1921, when at my home club in Bedford normally dignified retired Indian Army colonels were to be seen prostrate in mid-fairway, reaching down with a mashie-niblick at arm's length to retrieve balls from vast cracks.

Sometimes they not only failed to scoop up the ball but also dropped and lost their club, and then their rage was wonderful to see. I often think that archaeologists of later centuries may draw some very remarkable conclusions from the presence of these clubs buried twenty feet deep in the Bedfordshire clay.

We do not seem to have summers like those any more, or perhaps our fairways are more fertile. Either way it does not account for a man being 'carried', full pitch, at 300 yards. I cannot wait to see what Nicklaus & Co. will do—but one thing is certain. Even if he does 'destroy' the Old course, the rest of us never will.

Tied in Knots

I have long believed that golf and fly-fishing have much in common and that a man who enjoyed the former might well, as the years advanced, take readily to the latter. I am now putting the theory to the test—not, alas, the Test—and first impressions tend to prove it correct. The golfer-fisherman is not, after all, an uncommon species.

Horace Hutchinson, winner in 1886 and 1887 of the first two 'official' Amateur Championships and a writer and sculptor of considerable distinction, was a prominent member of the Houghton Club. The late Sir Harold Gillies painted the most beautiful pictures of fishing on the chalk streams and in Iceland. I once observed David Blair arriving for a Walker Cup match with fishing-rods protruding from his golf bag—in which, incidentally, there may somewhere lie the true definition of an amateur.

Another example is Sam Roberts, who played golf for Wales for more than twenty years and now runs a fishing lake in Flintshire. He has made a prolonged study of golf shafts and fishing rods and holds that their action has much in common. Having shown a beginner the rudiments of fly-casting, he asked him later how he was getting on. 'Not very well,' was the reply, 'but it has greatly improved my golf.' I only hope I shall be able to say the same.

In fishing I have already made, though I say it, quite a

few absolutely perfect casts and, as in the occasional perfect shot which all of us hit in golf, they were completely painless. No trouble at all. It is, as I say, the bad shots that are difficult. On examining the gut, for instance, I detected, close to the fly, two small knots.

Could the world's most expert fisherman, I wonder, cause a fly, invisible ten yards behind him, to whisk itself round and neatly tie a knot? Lashing a cigarette out of the lady's mouth on the stage with a stockwhip has nothing on the skill required to do this—on purpose. Again, anyone can cause the fly to hit the rod on the backswing. It takes a good man, though, to hook it, as I have done, in the quarter-inch ring at the far end of the shaft.

I suppose the most fatal words in both pastimes, even though unspoken, are 'got it at last!' After a series of particularly gratifying casts to the far side of the river, one of which secured a fine fat trout, I confess that they entered my head last week. The next moment I was groping for the reading glasses to unravel such a birds' nest of line and cast as eventually drove me to cut the damn thing off and start again.

On the golfing side Roberts believes that the camera cannot lie and that the action pictures one sees of 'bent' shafts are not due to distortion but are true. Sometimes one sees the shaft apparently bending forward at the moment of impact and this he believes to be evidence of a hook.

He maintains that no real power can be put into a stroke unless the shaft bends backwards, like a fly-rod, before the crucial moment of hitting and that few people in middle age retain their youthful power to bend the shaft on the downswing in this way. Thus we should all use progressively whippier shafts as we grow older.

Early experience shows that in both arts it is much more 'difficult' to play a bad shot than a good one. Bill Cox is probably the world's leading practitioner in socketing, or shanking, a golf ball. Indeed, I once saw him demonstrating a series of the most appalling sockets just before a competition, his theory being that you will never socket by mistake if you can socket on purpose.

Naturally, I sought instruction and was told that it was simple. All you had to do was to try to hit the ball with the end of the shaft. I invite you to try this. It is fantastically difficult. It took me ten, as I thought, grotesquely distorted strokes, most of which produced excellent shots, and it was only by trying to miss the ball completely on the far side that I at last achieved a socket. How one could ever do this by mistake defies imagination.

In golf and fishing we are allowed any number of practice swings before we play the shot that counts. Why is it that, when the moment comes, we cannot go through the same motions but have to give it that extra something? The ball goes out of bounds. The fly catches in the very tip of the only thistle in the field.

'Wait for it. Don't snatch,' the expert tells the novice, and here the fisherman has, I think, something to offer the golfer and, after letting it run through my head, I cannot wait to try it on the course. As you cast, you say to yourself slowly: 'Ladies—and—*Gentle*men.'

Another slogan is to say, when a fish rises, 'God Save the *Queen*' and not to strike till the word 'Queen', but this demands a power of self-control which I cannot yet command. It is not a thing at which I get enough practice.

Immortal Bobby

Till the age of six, when he first swung a golf club, Bobby Jones was a sickly child. At the age of forty-six he was stricken by a crippling ailment of the spine. In the intervening forty years he became undisputedly the world's greatest golfer and won for himself a degree of esteem and even affection which I imagine to be almost unequalled in sport.

Last week I received from him, long promised and long awaited, a copy of the book on which he has been labouring for the past two years. He has called it *Golf is My Game*, and I trust that in due course it will be published here.[1]

'I know,' he says almost in the opening paragraph, 'that my physical affliction was not derived in any sense from playing the game.' And yet I wonder. Though not tall, Jones was sturdily built. In his superbly graceful swing he reached positions which many of us could not attain with the aid of pulleys—his left arm straight as a ramrod high above his head on the backswing, and his right arm high and straight on the follow through.

A friend of mine watched him at Hoylake, where he won the second 'leg' of his great Grand Slam in 1930, in company with a doctor. 'Well,' said the doctor after a while, 'I am sorry, but I do not see how the human spine can stand that

[1] Chatto and Windus, 1961.

sort of thing for ever.' Jones should know best, but I have often wondered whether the doctor was right.[1]

The first 'leg' of the Grand Slam was the British Amateur Championship at St. Andrews, and Jones describes it as 'the most important tournament of my life'. It looked as though the highlight was to be Jones *v* Tolley on the Wednesday, but each had to dismiss two opponents first. One of Jones's was Sid Roper, the Nottingham artisan. Roper gave him a tremendous game and now, thirty years later, he receives one of the most heart-warming tributes I have read in golf.

One of those accursed well-wishers, who come up and say, 'Oh, you'll beat *him* all right', had assured Jones that Roper would probably do no hole in fewer than five. 'I had always held a notion,' says Jones, 'that I could make a pretty fair appraisal of the worth of an opponent simply by speaking to him on the 1st tee and taking a good, measuring look into his eyes.

'What I observed of Mr. Roper in this respect was not at all reassuring. He had a clear, steady look in his eyes; his manner and his bearing were quite composed, and he had the look not only of a competitor but of a golfer as well. When he struck his first tee shot, he looked even more like both. . . .'

Roper started with five fours, which is one under par. Jones began 3, 4, 3, 2, 4, which is five under par. When they finished, Jones needed two fours for a 68, including a stymie, and Roper had done 15 out of 16 holes in four. 'I think he

[1] Later, however, Jones wrote to me '. . . Regarding the observation of your doctor friend at Hoylake, I think I should tell you that according to the diagnosis most acceptable to me, golf had nothing to do with my present disability. It is not, as has so often been written, the result of arthritis or of a deformed or injured spinal structure. The diagnosis calls it syringomyelia. It is said to be a slow growth of fibrous tissues in the spinal cord itself. These tissues are horn-shaped, hence the "syringo". My doctors say that the best evidence is that, although the disease is not in-herited, the weakness or tendency exists at birth, but does not completely manifest itself till middle life.'

would have won from any other player in the field that day,'
says Jones, 'and I know that he would have beaten me on
any other day.'

Jones's match with Tolley has lived on as one of the classics
of match-play golf. 'Never,' wrote Bernard Darwin, 'was
there more perceptible the silence of expectation, the lull
before the storm in which men speak instinctively in
whispers.'

The match included one shot, Jones's second to the seventeenth, which is talked of to this day. He played deliberately
to the left, towards the 18th tee, and his ball hit a spectator
and stopped—the gallery not being confined behind the wall
as they are today.

'Hundreds,' to quote Darwin again, 'are prepared to take
the oath that it would otherwise have been on the road, and
an equal number of witnesses are quite certain that it would
not.' Tolley, forced to go for the green, caught the Road
bunker and then, with the flag between him and the road,
played a stroke which Jones still feels 'has never been surpassed for exquisitely beautiful execution'.

'I shall carry to my grave the impression of the lovely
little stroke with which he dropped the ball so softly in
exactly the right spot, so that, in the only possible way, it
finished dead to the hole. Tolley himself, after the passage
of twenty-eight years, confirmed to me that it was the finest
shot of his life. I am sure it was.'

Aided by a stymie, Jones won on the nineteenth and in
the following autumn, on the eleventh green at Merion, Pa.,
he shook hands with Eugene Homans, winner now of the
Open and Amateur Championships of Britain and the United
States all in one year.

Thirty years later almost to the day, I was privileged to
watch him lean from his wheel-chair beside this same green
to unveil a tablet commemorating his feat.

'*Golf is My Game*'

Here, from the world's greatest golfer, I have been

discovering much that will hearten us all. In an age where we now have to pay for other people's children to be given lessons, individually or *en masse*, it is revealing to learn that Jones never had a lesson in his life.

Like other great tournament players of his generation, most of whom started as caddies, he was 'turned out to pasture with a club or two and a few balls'. 'They learned to play golf, just as others learned baseball,' he says, 'by playing and playing and playing because they liked the game.'

His own model was the little Carnoustie-born professional to his home club at Atlanta, Stewart Maiden, who, as befitted his origin, had the old-fashioned, flowing Scottish swing. 'His method,' Jones remembers, 'was simple. It seemed that he merely stepped up to the ball and hit it, which to the end of my playing days was always a characteristic of my play.' Those who are lucky enough to have seen Jones's films in the 'thirties—and how I wish they would show them again!—will confirm how true this was.

When Jones was 'off', he went back to Maiden, who would simply indicate the 'point of basic disturbance'—and walk away. 'It seems obvious to me,' he says, 'that writing about the golf swing has become too technical and complicated, and even the most earnest teaching professional presents the game to his pupil as a far more difficult thing than it really is.'

This at once reminded me of a coincidence which I have always found irresistibly comical, though I did not like to say so at the time. In Hogan's great book *Power Golf* one of the first things I noticed was a full-page illustration, by that gifted professional illustrator of anatomy, Anthony Ravielli, of a golfer stripped, as it were, of his outer flesh and dressed only in his muscles. An almost identical drawing—though, with great respect to my old friend, Colonel Frank Wilson, not quite so professionally done—appeared in Stephen Potter's original *Gamesmanship* book, as an exercise in how to put your opponent off!

Here is another of Jones's views which I find stimulating. We are all agreed, I imagine, that the way to rest a tired or busy mind is not to set it thinking of nothing but to divert its attention to something else. This is when golf, as Jones puts it, is such an effective agent of mental therapy, since 'golfers know, and have known for a long time, that when playing golf it is almost impossible to think of anything else'.

In his view, therefore, we are detracting from our own ends when we urge people to 'relax, take it easy, be casual and carefree on the course'. He thinks we should do just the opposite, duffers and experts alike. What we really seek from the game can only be had by a concentration on the business in hand sufficiently intense to sweep away the problems, worries and troubles of everyday life.

When I think of myself ambling round, admiring the scenery, telling my friends I only play when the weather is right, chatting of this and that, hooking balls into the gorse bushes and not really caring, I am convinced that the great man is right and intend to mend my ways. Let my opponents beware from now on!

Finally the old, old problem of 'Then and Now'. Which was the greater? Grace or Hobbs, Hobbs or Bradman, Ball or Hilton, Vardon or Jones, Jones or Hogan? The list is endless and so is the argument. We all know that you cannot fairly compare men who competed against entirely different people under entirely different conditions and with different weapons—but still it goes on.

Jones, I think, has the final word and, like most of Sir Winston's utterances that will remain as quotations in the history books in a hundred years' time, it comes mainly in words of one syllable. 'I think we must agree,' he says, 'that all a man can do is to beat the people who are around at the same time that he is. He cannot win from those who came before, any more than he can win from those who come afterward.'

And that, at long last, seems to settle that.

Come off it, Gentlemen!

With the greatest respect to our friends across the Atlantic, I long ago came to the conclusion that almost every American influence on the game of golf, when it arrives in this country—and they all do in the end—should be resisted. I include the gigantic cabin-trunk bags (which professionals now use as advertisement hoardings for the firms whose products they are paid to use), the electric carts to carry the gigantic bags, the four-balls in which everyone holes out and which, therefore, take five hours, and, not least, those ghastly jockey caps.

Golf is now by many millions of dollars the biggest sporting business in America and, if you add the real estate connected with the 5,000 odd courses, it even dwarfs the Standard Oil of New Jersey, which is saying something. At the same time the golfer himself—and not only the American golfer at that—is the universal sucker of sport. He will clutch at what the slightest intelligence would tell him to be a straw, if it is suggested that it would add five yards to his drive.

He would cheerfully give a month's income for anything guaranteed to take two strokes a round off his game. He will try any short cut, hint or tip, however patently daft it may be.

With so much in his pocket and so little in his head, it is little wonder that the golfer is surrounded by people making the most extraordinary claims for their wares and inventing every day some new gadget or refinement whereby to extract his money. For many years I have been saying, in the hope of raising a laugh, that one day someone would start selling Americans head covers for their iron clubs as well as the woods. You have guessed? Yes, they are here. Four dollars 98 for a set of nine, including your initials. And for another $10 you can have a bag in which to carry your golf bag when you are not playing. And in a few years time, doubtless, a bag in which to carry the bag with your bag in it.

Since every golfer would sell the clothes off his wife's back in return for extra length, it is natural that every ball in America is alleged to go farther than every other: one because it has 'accelerator thread'; Hogan's because it is the only one with 'flash reaction'; another because it accelerates (presumably without the accelerator thread) to 170 m.p.h. more quickly than the others; another because of its fibre-glass centre, which makes it so long as to be almost unfair against people using balls filled with steel, rubber or liquid.

All this is good fun in its way, and indeed I derive much pleasure from my ever-increasing collection of lunatic golf advertisements—which, rightly or wrongly, assume our American friends to be the most credulous people in the world—but this is a catching disease and seems rapidly to be spreading to this country. In other words, people are beginning to try on you and me, and this is something up with which we should not put.

Nobody has ever taken more trouble in designing clubs than Ben Hogan, and if he tells me they are good I will believe him. The following, which I take from the advertisement of his clubs made in this country, I will not believe: 'A long time ago I realized that a perfect shot, even from the finest player, is a great rarity. Recognizing that this is caused by the variation in the swing from stroke to stroke I have tried to engineer into these clubs the maximum of what might be defined as the positive tendency of the clubs to swing correctly despite human error.'

If this appalling piece of jargon means anything, it means

237

that the great man is seriously asking me to believe that he has invented a sort of self-correcting club which will do the right thing, even though I do the wrong. If he has, he will save the sufferings of millions and should at once be made a life peer. If not—well, come off it, Ben!

Others tend to blind us with pseudo-science. Spaldings, for instance, who also make fine clubs, say of their 'woodless woods' (made of 'Terpolymite, the greatest aid to distance since the high compression ball') that they are possessed of 'Dimensional Micro-Stability'—which I am sure is a great advantage, though I should be surer still if I knew what it meant.

These clubs also have 'power-packed resiliency equivalent to the highest impact face insert—a sharp 'distance-click' no matter where club-face meets ball.' And so, at £7 17s. 6d. a time, they ought.

All the same, I am prepared to bet my friend Mr. Ralph Sammell, the managing director, a large whisky that I can hit a ball with one of his clubs with no 'distance-click' at all.

Nor shall another club-making friend of mine, Mr. John Letters, escape—if only for bringing back memories I was just beginning, through the acquisition of a croquet-mallet putter, to forget. For many years I had one of his centre-shafted putters 'whose well-known bronzed head may be seen on nearly every golf course in the world'. In the end I had only to set eyes on a four foot putt for the well-known bronzed head to develop a violent twitch and shoot forward before I was ready, at the same time turning slightly sideways. As for the shaft, it became more like trying to putt with an eel.

And what does Mr. Letters say of this loathsome weapon, at which I shudder every time I see it in the hallstand? He says, 'It gives an extraordinary sense of supreme confidence!' No, no. Come off it, gentlemen!

Postscript

I have a minor apology to make. Not the kind that results

from letters starting 'Dear Sir, my attention has been drawn . . .etc.' (the writer being in fact a constant reader and having seen it perfectly well for himself) but entirely unsolicited, out of the goodness of my heart and, so long as it costs nothing, my well-known sense of fair play. The recipient is Mr. Ralph Sammell, managing director of the firm that makes 'woodless woods' from a plastic substance named 'Terpolymite'.

Two or three months ago, in endeavouring to take the mickey out of some of the advertisements, mostly American, for modern golf equipment, I mentioned the claim for these clubs that they gave 'a sharp distance-click no matter where club-face meets ball'. I went so far as to offer to bet Mr. S. a large whisky that I could hit a ball with one of his clubs with no distance-click at all.

I still have not hit a ball with one of his clubs, but have been presented in the meantime with a trial set of a similar plastic-headed variety known as the 'Crookshank'—so-called because of the wry-neck which brings the face of the club in line with the shaft and may within ten years be standard practice all over the world. The result has astonished me. Hitherto, I should always have backed myself to tell a good shot with my back turned, simply from the noise it made. Not so any longer. These clubs do, indeed, have a 'distance-click'.

Everyone will recognize the drive which, hit right off the toe of the club, stings like the devil, falls 40 yards short, but at the same time to the outward eye has a correct trajectory. I doubt whether this was possible with hickory shafts, but it is a commonplace today and has become almost my standard tee-shot on the few occasions when I don't open the face. Normally it makes a wretched, dull sound, far removed from the sharp click of the well-struck ball.

Now all is different and for those prepared to deceive themselves alive the change is much for the better. From the acoustic point of view every shot is a good one, the noise being akin to that relayed on the television when the microphone beside the tee is set a bit too much 'up'. To the man who is honest with himself, however, it is a source of constant, though not wholly uncongenial, frustration.

No matter how you hit the ball, or so it seems, you do get the sharp 'distance-click'. Your fingers may be numbed by the impact and the ball stop feebly short of where it might have been, but 'Good shot!' they say, 'Good shot!', and then very soon 'Mind if I have a go with one of those clubs?' You cannot keep saying, 'I never hit it, really'. The answer is that you have got the click at last—but where, oh where, is the distance? In fairness I should add that when you do hit them, you get the click and the distance, and this is bliss indeed.

As a postscript regarding my plastic woods, not only do they make the noise of a good shot when you hit a bad one, but they also, when you come 'over and round' instead of 'under and through' to such an extent as to leave white paint—the mark of shame—on the snout of the club, enable you to erase it hastily with a moistened finger before anyone else can see it.

Treasure Trove

Some time ago a reader kindly sent me a 1907 copy of C. B. Fry's Magazine—*Of Action and Outdoor Life*—and I found it so refreshing, vigorous and intriguing by comparison with what may now be found on the bookstalls that I ventured, in writing about it here, to ask whether anyone had any further numbers that I could borrow.

One response, in handwriting that at once betrayed the writer's scholarly profession, came from an ex-housemaster of Eton, Mr. B. G. Whitfield, who, as it turned out, infuriates and bedevils so many thousands of readers each week as a compiler of the *Sunday Times* Crossword. Not only did he possess bound copies of every issue of Fry's magazine that was ever printed but he wished me to accept them as a gift. He would like them, he said, to 'go to a good home'.

For the past week, rationed to a volume a day, they have been my companions during the annual period of voluntary starvation and I have been living in a different and, as it seems, a simpler and better world, as it was at the time of my own entry into it. For sixpence you can buy the novels of Conan Doyle, Rider Haggard, Eden Phillpotts, Robert Hichens and a host of others; for 12 guineas you can have a first-class passage and a week in Las Palmas and for 22 the same in Jamaica. A firm in Hackney Wick is 'specially distilling petrol, the best spirit for motors'. Green's *Short History of the English People* is just beginning in forty parts at 7d. each and Shackleton is about to serialize his adventures in search of the South Pole.

Golf, I am glad to say, is widely featured by Fry, the master cricketer. In some ways it seems almost a primitive version, and none the worse for that, of the game we know today. In others, perhaps the more important, one knows that it will never change. Every week we have an article by Bernard Darwin, who was to continue writing as urbanely as ever for another forty years. 'With the month of April,' he exults, 'the blessed time of three rounds a day will have arrived.'

As was, and ever will be, length was every golfer's goal. The mightiest hitters in the land, regardless of handicap, were invited to contribute their secrets, but, as they bore little or no resemblance to each other, I have, alas, little of value to pass on.

The ball makers were, of course, as sure they knew the answer then as they are today. 'The Buzzard,' it was cheerfully claimed, 'the core being made of a Secret Substance, drives 20 yards further than other balls.' Another strongly recommended was the Kite—or the Baby Kite, 'best for wind and keen greens', precursor of the small *v.* big ball controversy of today. To present manufacturers, however, I would specially commend the Corinthian—24s. a dozen and 'a free one, just to play for'.

One of the joys of my early golfing life was repainting balls. Do people do it now, I wonder? It was quite an art, albeit a messy one. You smeared the paint on your palms— I can smell it now—rubbed the balls round and round to get an even surface and set them to dry on a sort of fakir's bed of nails. They did it better in earlier times, with Groom's Patent Clip and Drying Tray, wherewith you held the ball with one of those clips with which today you dip eggs into preservative and painted it with a brush. The whole outfit, 3s. 6d., highly commended by Harry Lauder.

Into the respective merits of, say, Palmer and Vardon, I will not enter, but a match I should dearly love to see would be the two of them at the same age, using Vardon's clubs and balls and wearing Vardon's clothes. Here surely we may claim to have 'progressed'.

What fun, too, and this time entirely practicable, to stage a match between two of the leading ladies of today, attired in the clothes of yesterday—including the elastic 'Miss Higgins' to contain the billowings of the voluminous skirt. I see a picture of one such, with patent leather slippers peeping coyly forth. 'The lady who endeavours to sooth overstrung nerves by violent exercise,' says the caption, 'usually accentuates the trouble and eventually breaks down entirely.' Not, I fancy, today.

It is nice to think that there was a time when a man could seriously write 'thus far the younger class of American golfers seem to have the modern ailment of 'nerves', and to be erratic in consequence in their play'. Americans have changed with a vengeance, but the lure of the game is eternal. As true today as when it was written is the anonymous enthusiast's 'Not until death has holed him out does the golfer abandon his search after the perfect game'.

'What Club do I Throw?'

Golfers are not what they were. When I began the game, the public image of the golfer was that of a red-faced, white-moustached, plus-foured gentleman, presumably a colonel (Indian Army, rtd.) hacking away in a bunker and uttering appalling and unprintable oaths. Now all, or nearly all, is sweetness and light, so much so that in the best circles you do not even knock your opponent's ball away when you concede him a putt. Instead, you pick it up and with elaborate courtesy walk across the green and place it in his hand.

The thoughts occurred to me because I have just chanced upon details of a rather splendid competition which was staged at the Druid Hills course, at Atlanta, Georgia, before the war and recorded by Bobby Jones's 'Boswell', the late O. B. Keeler. From time to time, people are kind enough to write to me and ask whether I can suggest any different form of competition with which to interest the members of their clubs. This might be the answer.

It appears that Harry Stephens, who was then professional at the Druid Hills Club, in the course of reading the riot act to a junior member whom he had observed throwing a club, said, 'One of these days I'm going to put on a club-throwing contest to show you boys just how stupid you really look.' The idea took root and the contest was duly staged. I would rather have witnessed it than many a solemn tournament of today.

After a couple of practice days, part of the first fairway was duly marked out with an out-of-bounds area on either side. Sixty contestants turned up, old and young, and there were prizes of three golf balls for different events calling for distance, altitude or accuracy, for left-handers and right-handers. The first question that arose, before any consideration of style or method, was: 'What club do I throw?'

Instinct would have led me to put my faith in a good, solid driver. In fact, the most effective weapon proved to be that which, I imagine, is most often thrown in earnest, namely the putter.

Each player—for the benefit of anyone who may wish to promote such a contest, possibly on the morning after the club dinner, was allowed three shots, as in a long-driving competition, and some of the results were far from orthodox.

The professional himself, whirling round in the fashion of a man throwing the hammer, released his missile at the wrong moment and it pitched in the club-house veranda, fortunately without killing anyone. Several others, presumably right-handers, hooked out of bounds.

The results, judging by memories of my own club-throwing days and the efforts of some of my friends were, I think, remarkable. How far would you back yourself to fling a golf club? I should have thought the length of two cricket pitches would represent something like a handicap of scratch. This, however, would have turned out to be very much of an also-ran.

The right-handed winner achieved a magnificent throw of 61 yards. The accuracy award went to a man who flung a mashie-niblick within seven feet eight inches of a marker at 50 yards, while the altitude record was set by a player who hurled a pitching iron about 20 feet over the top of an 80-foot pine tree.

Golf is the most infuriating of all games, with the possible exception of ludo—which I have recently resumed after all too long an interval—and I am not sure that we get the best out of it by bottling up our emotions for the sake of etiquette. I have always had a sneaking sympathy with Tommy Bolt, who is constantly being fined or suspended in America for throwing or breaking clubs or for other conduct calculated to cause a breach of the golfing peace.

I am not, I hope, libelling that elder statesman of Australian professional golf, Norman von Nida, when I recall that in his more explosive days he threw his putter over the railway line at Southport and Ainsdale.

Far and away the finest example, however, was afforded by the late Lord Castlerosse, friendship with whom remains among the richer experiences of my life. We had played at Walton Heath and his lordship had not been in form. Not less than a dozen times, including on the 18th tee, he hit his ball into the heather and simply instructed his caddie 'Pick it up'.

As we approached the last green, he called for a club and ball. The shot narrowly missed his left leg and scuttled into the heather. With supremely aristocratic disdain he tossed the club to the ground and, marching off, said over his shoulder to the caddie, 'Pick that up. Have the clubs destroyed. And leave the course!'

The Old Gutty-Puncher

One Sunday I reproduced in facsimile the beginning of a letter written to me in such a flawless and unwavering copperplate hand as to draw it at once to one's attention.

It would take you a long time, I fancy, to guess the age of the writer of this letter. He is in fact ninety-two and he is John Rowe, who lives within a few hundred yards of the Royal Ashdown Forest Golf Club from which he retired in 1947. He had served as their professional for fifty-five years.

John Rowe reminisces as clearly as he writes and to find so distinct a link with the really distant past has been, to me, a great delight. He might have been a champion, had he practised instead of devoting himself to the art of club-making—an art which came naturally to him since, his mother having declared that she would 'rather be in her grave than see him become a golf professional', he was for six years apprenticed to a carpenter.

In his early days they made wooden clubs from beech, or occasionally apple—'scores of 'em at 4s. 6d., boy. If we got 5s. 6d. we reckoned we were getting on.' I wonder whether any club-maker alive today has gone out into the forest, as Rowe did, and selected and purchased a whole beech tree? The poorer the soil, and the more buffeting it had had from the wind, the slower it grew and, therefore, the better it was for the purpose.

One of the points of his letter was to show me a newspaper cutting of 1888, pointing out that the revolutionary 'three halves and seven forwards' formation used by the New Zealand 'All Blacks', at that time visiting Britain was nothing new. The Northam Colts, of Westward Ho!—full-back J. Rowe and among the forwards J. H. Taylor—had been using it for years!

From that team of fifteen no fewer than seven became golf professionals. In addition to Rowe and 'J. H.' there were Jack and William Hutchings, who went to Derby; George Cawsey (Malvern and Birmingham); William Fulford (Northwood); and John Horrill, who joined Rowe as assistant at Ashdown Forest. When they left, that was the end of the Northam Colts.

'My dear Boy,' he writes breezily, 'I wonder if you can realize what a gang we were. All golfers, nearly all bell-ringers, all footballers and cricketers, and mostly all swimmers. Will any of the poor topnotch golfers of today be able to look back on such an interesting and varied life as we had?'

A pretty rigorous life too. Every morning, he told me during an intriguing couple of hours I spent with him, he walked three miles to be at work by 6.30. With half an hour for dinner, he worked till 6 p.m.—for the princely sum of 3s. 6d. a week, rising a shilling a year to 8s. 6d.—and then in the summer walked home, had a hasty cup of tea, ran a mile to the links and played golf till it was too dark to see.

The first heroes he saw in a tournament at Westward Ho! have receded, even for my generation, into legend. The mighty-hitting Douglas Rolland, for instance, who, when the others with their gutty balls could only just make the 170-yard carry over the big bunker at the fourth and then needed a wood for their seconds, carried the bunker by 60 yards and got on with a mashie; and Jack Burns, who, after winning the Open in 1888, retired to his original job as a platelayer on the railway and made the immortal observation that he was 'never off the line now'.

In the interval between carpentering and becoming a golf professional, Rowe studied at an art school, and on his wall are some really exquisite designs that won him a diploma. Another of his treasures is a 1747 map of the Forest presented to him when he retired after twenty-nine years as a Conservator.

He ends his letter with 'Now, here I am, an antiquated and fossilized old gutty-puncher looking back and thankful to think that I have known golf when it was a game full of kindness between employer and employee and wondering whether the world will ever be the same again. So long, boy.'

And as he showed me out of his home, he said, in the broad West Country accent that has never deserted him, 'Well, I've had a good run, boy. I've had a good run.' A very fine run indeed, if I may say so, and a much respected one at that.[1]

---

[1] Soon afterwards Rowe wrote me another letter, in the same copperplate hand. 'Well,' it concluded, 'I'm coming up to the last green now, boy.' Within a month or two he had reached it.

David and the Two Goliaths

'Morning dawned with a steady, drizzling rain still falling and a gloomy white mist hanging here and there, and the ground was soft, greasy and muddy. Nothing, however, could damp the enthusiasm of the spectators, who came pouring out of Boston long before 10 o'clock. Brookline, with its rolling hills, valleys and jutting promontories of rock, made a most dramatic setting for the great match, ridge after ridge being capped with a great crowd of onlookers. The red flags bowed tumultuously up and down the hills. Tenors, basses and baritones shouted themselves hoarse through megaphones. Rope men worked like tigers. To hear the crowd thundering behind gave a realistic and alarming feeling of leading a cavalry charge.

'The crowd behaved admirably and was most generous and impartial. It did its best not to applaud too much nor too loud for its own man, but complete restraint would have been more than human. When Mr. Ouimet with a good putt on the seventeenth green put himself three strokes ahead of Vardon, there was such an outburst of cheers, yells and catcalls as no one who heard it is ever likely to forget.'

Thus wrote Bernard Darwin in *The Times* of 22 September 1913, reporting on perhaps the greatest day in the history of American golf. This was the replay at the Country Club for the U.S. Open Championships between the two British giants, Vardon and Ray, and a twenty-year-old local lad called Francis Ouimet, whose name the golfing public did not even know how to pronounce. It is in fact '*We* met'.

Francis was the son of a working man who had a modest house adjacent to the Country Club and no interest in golf. His elder brother supplemented the family income by caddying at the club and when he was old enough, i.e. eleven, Francis did the same. They collected lost balls, as boys with sharp eyes will, and when they had accumulated three dozen exchanged them in a shop for a mashie and, later, another 36 for a brassie. With these two clubs Francis practised surreptitiously on the course in the early morning, until the arrival of the green-keepers put him to flight.

When he was twenty, he won the State Amateur Championship and had succeeded, for the first time in four efforts, in qualifying for the National Amateur. This was about the full extent of his achievements when he entered for the Open—largely because it was played opposite his front door.

Arrayed against him were not only Vardon and Ray, but the full flower of American professional golf, including among others Jim Barnes, later to win the British Open, who Darwin observed, 'has rather long hair and a loose, dashing carriage and gives to British eyes a suggestion of the Wild West, but is in fact an Englishman from Cornwall'.

When the last day started in pouring rain, Vardon and Wilfred Reid, of Banstead Downs, England, were tied at 147, two ahead of Ray (who had at first 'showed a deplorable preference for the trees, with the result that 5's and 6's were horribly prevalent'), three ahead of Macdonald Smith and Barnes, and four ahead of Ouimet and another young fellow, Walter Hagen. At the end of the morning round Ouimet (74) had caught Vardon and Ray, and the three were tied at 225.

Vardon and Ray each then took 79 and Ouimet was out in 43. He pulled up to such good purpose that he needed to cut one stroke off the par of 3, 4, 4 for the last three holes to tie. He did it by holing a long putt at the seventeenth and knocking a 5-footer calmly in at the eighteenth. It was as though, today, the county champion of Fife tied with Nicklaus and Palmer in the Open at St. Andrews.

Next day all three went out in 38. Gradually Ray dropped from the picture at the fifteenth and with two to play Ouimet, complete master of himself, was one stroke ahead of Vardon. It was then that he holed his historic putt on the seventeenth for a 3 against Vardon's 5.

When he tapped in his last putt, having come home in the astonishing figure of 34, he was 'straightway whirled off his feet and carried shoulder high off the green, leaving even the most patriotic Americans gasping at the brilliance of their young champion and the greatness of his victory'. Ouimet 72, Vardon 77, Ray 78.

Bernard Darwin, who was marking Ouimet's card—it hangs framed in the club-house today—went into ecstasies. 'Far the most enthralling game of golf I have ever seen . . . an exhibition of skill, nerve and courage that have never been equalled . . . one David against two Goliaths . . . wore his men down and finally battered and trampled on them . . . if I could find stronger language I should certainly use it.'

So Francis became overnight a national hero and the supremacy of the British was broken for ever. He played in or captained every American Walker Cup team till after the war and in 1951 the Royal and Ancient Club accorded him the highest honour within their power to bestow by making him their captain. In the middle of his speech at the dinner he stopped and slowly said, 'It may interest you to know, gentlemen, that it is thirty-eight years ago *this day* that I beat Vardon and Ray.' It was one of the most moving moments I can remember.

[A week after writing this I had the honour of attending a dinner given for Ouimet at the Country Club, where the U.S. Open was appropriately being played, to celebrate the 50th anniversary of his great feat.]

The Fine Scotch Game of Golf

'Eighteen Sixty Four,' wrote Bernard Darwin, 'is not very long ago in the history of the world, but it is very long ago in the history of golf in England.' The year in question marks, in fact, the birth of the 'North Devon and West of England Golf Club' at Westward Ho!—now the Royal North Devon—and this year, 1964, they become the first club in England to play continuously on the same course for a hundred years.

This is situated on the flat expanse of 'linksland' which stretches from the village of Northam to the Pebble Ridge and is known as the Burrows.

It was here that General Moncrieff made his celebrated remark that it was 'evidently designed by providence for a golf links'. The General himself came from St. Andrews and so, of course, did Tom Morris, who came down to re-arrange the early course, but Westward Ho! was the first and, later with Hoylake, the greatest of the truly English clubs.

The pious founder, the Rev. I. H. Gosset, was a Devon man and so were those who attended the first meeting 'to arrange the preliminaries of a golf club for playing the fine Scotch game of golf on the Burrows at Northam'.

What trouble they would have been in today when, for a reason that to me remains wholly unaccountable, whisky, salmon, tape, beef, sea mists and, I daresay, one or two other commodities are Scotch but to refer to a game or, worse still, a man as Scotch, instead of Scottish or, worse, Scots, is regarded as a deadly national insult.

The simple, elementary amenities of course and club-house which satisfied the gentlemen golfers of early days have always fascinated me, perhaps because my own first introduction to the game was on three unmarked holes on Yelverton Common. At Westward Ho!, the great Horace Hutchinson recorded, they used to cut the hole with a dinner knife—what Army quartermasters, I seem to remember, call a 'nine-inch, cookhouse, large'—and when one hole became too dilapidated one of the players would get out his clasp knife and cut another. To tee your ball you took a pinch of sand from the bottom of the hole, which thus got deeper and deeper, until 'it often happened that one had to lie down so as to stretch one's arm at full length in order to reach the ball at the bottom of the hole'. To mark the hole they stuck in the feather of a rook or a gull.

Their first club-house was a room in a farm but they graduated to a bathing hut containing food and drink, which was dragged out to the 1st tee by coastguards. Then, till it was washed away, they had an iron hut on the Pebble Ridge and this was the setting for a scene surely without parallel in golfing history. They had, to quote Hutchinson again, 'many old Indian officers, with livers a little touched, who, when the golf ball would not obey their wishes with the same docility as the obedient Oriental, addressed it with many strange British words, which I delighted to hear, and yet stranger words in Hindustani, which I much regretted not to understand'.

One day a gallant but dissatisfied colonel was to be seen stark naked, picking his way daintily with unshod feet over the great boulders of the Pebble Ridge. He waded as far as possible out to sea and one by one cast his offending clubs beyond the farthest line of breakers. 'That the waves and tide were sure to bring them in again, to the delight of the salvaging caddies, made no matter to him. From him they were gone for ever and his soul was at rest.'

In the early days they played either seventeen or twenty-two holes and for a while the record for the long course was held by the Reverend Gosset with 149. With the increasing pressure on land space we may yet again see courses not with eighteen holes, for which there is really no valid reason, but simply with as many as will fit in.

Do we, I wonder, produce the same kind of 'characters' today? Such, for instance, as Captain G. F. M. Molesworth, R.N., familiarly known as the Old Mole, and the original of Colonel Dabney in *Stalky and Co*. He was wont to drive furiously over to the links from Bideford 'manipulating the reins in strictly professional style, the carriage going at the full speed of the horse and making very heavy weather of it over the ruts and bumps, and only the sailor's special Providence bringing them safe to port before the Iron Hut'.

It was in September, 1877, that the Old Mole took on a wager, the result of which remains arguable today. The terms were that he was to walk the three miles to the links, play six rounds in less than 660 strokes carrying his own clubs, and walk back, all between daylight and dark. He left home at 5.20 a.m., reached the Iron Hut at 6.0 a.m. and played the first 54 holes without stopping, in about the time that a transatlantic four-ball takes to play eighteen. The ninth hole cost him fourteen in the first round and fifteen in the third and his total for six rounds was 662.

Declining to yield, the Captain then played a seventh round in 104 and, leaving out the first, this gave him a total of 646—the winner by 14 shots. He had played the seven rounds in 11 hours 20 minutes and walked home by 6.40.

Controversy at once broke out. The Captain said that he had played six rounds in the day in under 660, had carried his own clubs and had walked to and from the course, all between daylight and dark, and it was therefore a case of 'Pay up, gentlemen'. The opposition declared that he had played six rounds and taken 662. 'A case will be drawn and the matter referred to,' said *The Field*. We are not, alas, told the verdict. What would yours have been? On the whole, I think I should have come against the Captain, though I should not have relished telling him so.

Nowadays Westward Ho! is considered to be somewhat out of the way and the Amateur Championship of 1931 will probably prove to be its last. It was won by my old friend and foursome partner, Eric Martin Smith, just down from Cambridge. As he reached the semi-final, he received a wire, widely but incorrectly attributed to myself, saying: 'Ridiculous, but stick to it.' He did.

To celebrate the Westwood Ho! centenary another Cambridge player, John Goodban, edited a most delightful anthology of writings and pictures relating to the club, which anyone who has enjoyed the ancient links can obtain from the secretary for 35s.—with the assurance that he will, in Darwin's words, 'Lose himself in a golden and sentimental mist of other people's memories and enjoy it prodigiously'.

The Universal Amateur

The death of Lord Brabazon of Tara will leave an absolutely unfillable gap in the lives of all who had the good fortune to know him. He was completely unique. His eighty years of life, ten better than the established par of three score and ten, covered more radical changes in human existence than any other two centuries put together and it seemed as though he was in at the birth of them all. He was the most 'interesting' man—in the sense of stimulating one's own interest—I ever met and I doubt whether anyone could remember having spent a dull moment in his company.

The walls of his office told his early story. Here, for instance, was Aviator's Certificate No. 1 of the Fédération Aeronautique Internationale, dated March 8, 1910—thirty years after which the holder started the craze for 'personal' car numbers by securing FLY 1.

Next to it a young man with gum boots, Norfolk jacket, and slightly prominent teeth is seen grasping the levers of a Heath Robinson flying machine—none other than the 'biplane pusher with bamboo and ash framework', which was the first all-English aeroplane to fly. With it Brab won £1,000 from the *Daily Mail* for a circular flight of one mile, average height 40 ft.

Another picture, surely a unique galaxy of aeronautical pioneers, shows, under the heading 'First English Aerodrome,

Mussel Manor, Shellbeach, Sheppey, 4 May, 1909', a knickerbockered group including all three of the Short brothers, Wilbur and Orville Wright, young Moore-Brabazon, and the handsome, ill-fated Charlie Rolls, of Rolls-Royce, whom Brab was later to see killed in an air display.

'The only gentleman's way of leaving the ground,' he used to say, 'is ballooning,' and in another picture he is standing in the basket with Charlie Rolls, waiting to ascend from Battersea Gasworks (45,000 cu. ft. £4 10s. 'including labour and bags of sand: holders-down extra'.)

Other pictures reveal him, in chauffeur's cap, waiting to crank the first Rolls-Royce, with the Duke of Connaught sitting bolt upright as passenger; and at the huge high steering wheel of the Minerva with which he won the Circuit des Ardennes in 1907.

Beside one of the most remarkable pictures ever taken of the Cresta toboggan run are, curiously enough, two of a main-line railway station. Only very close inspection reveals them to be models—reminders of younger days when Brab had the best model railway in England. He *would* have! He ran it with his brother-in-law, Clarence Krabbe, and when they had an accident they stopped and held an 'inquiry'. He would never travel by train without first inspecting the engine. 'Have you ever driven one of these?' he asked, as we were about to embark on a journey to Belgium. When I replied that I had not, he said, 'I'll tell you what it's like. It's like driving a very powerful sports car, with two big ends gone *and* a puncture.'

One day I chanced upon him at Turnberry, at breakfast, poring over what appeared to be a football pools coupon. It would have been in keeping with him if it had been, as he would have undoubtedly just worked out a completely novel system of permutations and combinations. As it happened, he was engaged in a chess match by post with Lady Powerscourt in Dublin and was filling in his next move. This was in mid-summer. I asked him how he was getting on. 'I lost a bishop in February,' he said, 'and have been in difficulties ever since.' I did not see him again till about September. I again asked him how he was getting on. He looked round with an almost conspiratorial air, as though to make sure that no one was listening, and said, 'I was mated last week.' We agreed that he might now add to his many other distinctions that of being the only peer ever to have been mated by post.

Among the many other 'firsts' in Brab's life was that, as a boy at Harrow, he was walking down Grove Hill when a few yards away from him a motorist put on the brakes too hard, ripped the spokes from his wheels, and became the first man to be killed in a motor accident. While others stood back, waiting for the infernal machine to blow up, Brab stepped forward and turned off the ignition burners. He was the only person who knew what they were. Afterwards he gave a lecture to the school scientific society on The Motor Car. 'A treasure now lost to the world,' he called it.

Brab was the complete pioneer. He was one of the earliest riders on the Cresta, and certainly, in his seventies, the oldest. In the first war he became without question the 'father' of modern air photography. He once turned up at Cowes with a kind of rotor arm attached to the mast instead of a sail. It was he who, somewhat ridiculed at the time, pulled the first trolley up the first fairway at St. Andrews.

Later he was to be led out by the past captains at 8 o'clock on a September morning to drive himself in down the same fairway, as captain of the Royal and Ancient. He had previously been observed making surreptitious practice swings in his shirt sleeves behind the bandstand, but, when he executed one or two on the 1st tee, I remember remarking to my companion that, if the real thing were to turn out like these, no great good could come of it.

In fact, he hit it all along the ground towards mid-wicket and the ball had long been stationary before the first of the caddies could reach it. Afterwards he described his opening stroke as a 'noble gesture of self-denial which has given pleasure to thousands'.

With his booming, unmistakable voice he would hold an audience anywhere, whether in the Commons, the Lords, after-dinner or, particularly, in the United States. Proposing the toast of the Open Champion at a dinner, he opened with: 'It is only appropriate that a Member of Parliament whose constituency borders upon Liverpool and Merseyside should be asked to get up on his hind legs and propose the toast of Cotton.'

It was he who in the Commons likened the Opposition to 'a lot of inverted Micawbers waiting for something to turn down'. Nor did his own side escape, for it was them, I seem to remember, that he meant when he referred to the 'snores of the Front Bench reverberating throughout the land'. It was certainly the then Archbishop of Canterbury whom he accused, when His Grace had made a speech on finance, of 'talking through his mitre'.

When Prince's, Sandwich, was used as a target range in the war, Brab declared that it was 'like throwing darts at a Rembrandt'. When Royal St. George's was waterlogged and too little, he thought, was being done about it, he put a suggestion in the book 'that the water in the bunker at the 13th be changed'.

People who worked with him were always astonished at the variety of subjects on which he could truly be described as expert. Yet in many ways he was an example of that rare, invaluable, and almost extinct species, the Universal Amateur.

Of the more serious side of Brab's long life—his work as Minister of Transport during the blitz and later of Aircraft Production, as President of the Royal Institution, and on the board of many eminent companies, I must leave it to others to write.

For those who pursue the humble game of golf, however, it is nice to think that a man of so many parts and of such immense distinction should have written in his autobiography, 'When I look back on my life and try to decide out of what I have got most actual pleasure, I have no doubt at all that I have got more out of golf than anything else'.